MW00619108

THE SFAS EMES

THE SFAS EMES

THE LIFE AND TEACHINGS OF
RABBI YEHUDA ARYEH LEIB ALTER

MOSHE A. BRAUN

JASON ARONSON INC.
Northvale, New Jersey
Jerusalem

This book was set in 11 pt. Souvenir by Alpha Graphics of Pittsfield, New Hampshire and printed and bound by Book-mart Press, Inc. of North Bergen, NJ.

10 9 8 7 6 5 4 3 2 1

Library of Congress Cataloging-in-Publication Data
Braun, Moshe A.
    The Sfas Emes : the life and teachings of Rabbi Yehudah Aryeh Leib
  Alter / Moshe A. Braun.
        p.   cm.
    Includes index.
    ISBN 0–7657–6005–3
    1. Alter, Judah Aryeh Leib, 1847–1905.   2. Rabbis—Poland—Góra
Kalwaria—Biography.   3. Hasidim—Poland—Góra Kalwaria—Biography.
4. Hasidism.   I. Title.
    BM755.A67B73   1998
    296.8'332'092—dc21   97-46203
    [B]   CIP

Printed in the United States of America. Jason Aronson Inc. offers books and cassettes. For information and catalog write to Jason Aronson Inc., 230 Livingston Street, Northvale, NJ 07647-1726, or visit our website: http://www.aronson.com

This volume is dedicated to the memory of

רחל ע״ה בת רב חיים ישעיהו נ״י

Ruchie Gruenburg ה״ע

אשת חיל מי ימצא

Fortunate are those who knew her. She shared her heart of pure gold with whomever she met. She seemed to have an endless supply of patience and strength.

With her trust in Hashem and her cheerful attitude, she was a role model for all of us with lesser cares.

She was devoted to all acts of charity. No cause was too large or an individual too small for her attention.

As a loving mother, devoted wife, and adoring grandmother, she had the encouraging word, empathetic ear, and supporting shoulder for all who needed her. Despite everything, she always had a warm smile and a kind word for everyone, radiating love and joy, true inner piety, quiet faith and fortitude, and a profound love for chesed.

קמו בניה ויאשרוה
בעלה ויהללה

Her Children arise and
praise her;
her husband, and he lauds
her.
(Proverbs 31.21)

Contents

A Note to the Reader

How to use this book

The reader should choose a topic from the table of contents and read one of the rebbe's teachings. He should then ask, "How can I apply this teaching to the place and people in my life at this moment? How can this teaching elevate me—my thoughts, speech, and actions—to a higher level of kindness, benevolence, and love? How can this teaching raise me to the next level of humility and God-consciousness? How can it help me to proceed further along the royal path with the servants of God?"

He should then spend some moments thinking and re-thinking the rebbe's teaching, and answering those questions.

If a difficult moral dilemma or other personal problem comes up, the reader can open the book at random, read one of the teachings on the page, apply it to his or her problem, and pray, "May it be the will of our Creator to grant me wisdom to see the solution within the problem. May I merit open eyes to reveal the concealment. Amen."

Introduction

About twenty years ago, I was absorbed in the writings of the Gerer Rebbe, Rabbi Yehudah Aryeh Leib Alter, better known as the Sfas Emes, a name coined by his children, meaning, "Lips of truth shall endure forever." (Proverbs 12:19) As a result of a desire to teach others, I was also translating his work into English and had finished two Torah portions, *Bereishis* and *Noah*, about one hundred pages of manuscript, by the year 1979.

One summer day of that year, the phone rang and it was a friend telling me that the Gerer Rebbe, Rebbi Simcha Bunim Alter, a grandson of the Sfas Emes, had arrived in New York from Israel, and anyone could see him and receive his blessings and some blessed fruit. It suddenly dawned on me that it would be an excellent opportunity to speak to the rebbe about my project and perhaps get assurances for its publication.

When I arrived at the Gerer *shtible*, it was mobbed with people trying to see the rebbe. I stood on line with the others and mentally prepared my conversation with answers to any objections the rebbe might have. I prayed to God to be with me and guide my lips to say the right words. Suddenly I was at the door, and I could already see the procedure. Some of the rather tall *hasidim* helped move the people along; as they came before the rebbe he placed two fruits into their waiting hands, and they were ushered out the door. Suddenly I was standing before the rebbe. He gave me the fruit, and then I said what I had been practicing to say for the preceding few minutes.

"May I speak a few words with the rebbe?" The rebbe looked a bit surprised and said, "*Nu*," meaning "go ahead."

"I work with intelligent young people who understand English better than Yiddish," I continued, "and I have been learning with them the Sfas Emes on the Torah. And they really like it; it is so refreshing and brilliant! Now I started to translate it," (and here I opened my folder to show the pages of the manuscript) "and I would like to publish it. It is a wonderful collection to inspire the youth hungry for the word of God. Especially nowadays that there is such a great awakening."

The rebbe looked at the manuscript then looked up at me and said, "Fine. Call my brother in *Eretz Yisroel* and he will take care of this project financially."

I couldn't believe my ears! The rebbe had opened a door for the book to get published, and with his help! I was elated. I thanked the rebbe very much and proceeded to leave the room. Walking out into the crowded hallway, I was greeted by several acquaintances, Gerer *hasidim*, who turned to me saying, "*Zolst hobben gepoylt alles gutts!*" ("You should have the merit to have accomplished!")

I had taken only a few steps when two tall *hasidim* rushed over to me and said, "The rebbe would like to see you!" When I turned to enter the rebbe's room, my heart sank. As I entered, I noticed a very grim look on the face of everyone in the room. I stood before the rebbe and he began by asking me, "What is your connection with the Sfas Emes? Are you a Gerer hasid?"

"No, I am not."

"What then?" the rebbe asked.

I replied, "I am not a Gerer hasid, yet I appreciate his deep teachings and realize what a wonderful source of inspiration his writings are, especially for young people seeking Torah."

"Still, to take his entire work and translate it? And into English? Why do you need to do that?" asked the rebbe.

"I understand the rebbe's concern," I said. "But we now have a wonderful opportunity to make his holy teaching available for those who are thirsting for its depth. And because they are less fluent in Hebrew, there is all the more reason to offer it to them."

"Yes, yes," the rebbe answered, "but there will be time when the Moshiach comes . . . ." And with that he motioned that the conversation was over, and I was ushered out of the room.

I was deeply disappointed by the rebuff and change of my fortunes. I walked out in a bit of a daze and went directly to see my very good friend, Rabbi Aryeh Kaplan, who lived nearby. I tearfully related to him what had just happened. He thought for a moment and said, "You know, Moshe, this is probably the best thing that could have happened! Well, you can't blame the Gerer for feeling that they are the protectors of the property titled 'the Sfas Emes'. After all, he was, and still is, their rebbe. But no one owns those teachings. Perhaps you would do better to stop translating the work of the Sfas Emes in their entirety. After all, in practical terms, you would end up with twenty volumes or more, and who would be able to afford something like that?! You would do much better, and reach more people, if you started writing a book based on his teachings, like a book on the holidays."

Suddenly the dark cloud that had been around my head disappeared, and a bright light shone through. "Why, I never thought of that!" I said. "That is a splendid idea!" I thanked Rabbi Kaplan, and after a brief conversation I departed. As soon as I got home, I started on my first book on the holidays, based on the Sfas Emes. After completing six of those books, I was very fortunate to gain the acquaintance of Arthur Kurzweil of Jason Aronson Publishers. He liked my work, and in 1996 published it in one large volume titled *The Jewish Holy Days*. Since then I have written two other books, *Pointing the Way* and *Sabbath Peace*. The present book is the ninth work I have written based on the teachings of the Sfas Emes.

The Sfas Emes shares his spiritual insights in his commentary on the Torah. Those are the thoughts studied in this book in detail. They are presented in lucid terms, to be used by the reader as springboards for meditation and study.

In addition, one cannot possibly appreciate the magnitude of the rebbe's genius without knowing more about this great personage. I have therefore included a number of stories about the Sfas Emes that illustrate how his life imitated his teachings. The anecdotes and the teachings together form an amalgam that the reader will not soon forget. And the great light possessed by this sage will leave us wiser, more able to live a life filled with wisdom and to add the warmth of the holy fire into our lives.

Acknowledgments

I would like to thank Arthur Kurzweil and the staff at Jason Aronson Inc. for a job well done! Also, a special thanks to Rabbi Efrayim Grossberger, Judaic historian and librarian, for his assistance.

I would also like to thank my dear wife, Leah, for her selfless devotion. She started me off on the first book and continued through this, my ninth book, based on the Sfas Emes. May her merit endure for our children: Zevy, Pessie, and Chevele; Shaindy, Sruly, Surala, Shmuel Zevy, Gitty, and Dovid Yitzchok Isaac; Mutty, Gitty, Yisroel Reuven, Chayala, and Yaakov Akiva; Chavy, Daniel, Yisroel, and Yehudah; Chaya Yitty and Yosef Yehudah Yitzchok Issac. May they all live with lips of truth.

Part I

The Sfas Emes:
His Life

$\mathcal{A}$ Tragic Past

The Grandfather of the Sfas Emes

The grandfather of the Sfas Emes was Rabbi Yitzchok Meir Roetenburg, a brilliant Torah scholar with unparalleled wisdom, and a devoted student and hasid of the Magid of Koznitz. The Magid recognized his student's greatness in scholarship, leadership, and purity of character. He decided that when he left the world he would leave his *hasidim* in the able hands of his beloved student.

To Pershischa

All was fine and well until Rabbi Yitzchok Meir heard stories about the greatness of Rebbe Bunim of Pershischa and decided to see for himself. He was deeply impressed and inspired and immediately knew that the root of his soul was connected with the soul of his new teacher. But how could he leave his beloved teacher, the Magid? He returned to the Magid and there spent days mulling over his decision. In the end he decided that to reach his full potential he had to leave the Magid and study with Rebbe Bunim. His friends tried to dissuade him, but he had already made up his mind, and he left.

After staying with Rebbe Bunim for several weeks, he started homeward with a great feeling of satisfaction. Unfortunately a tragedy awaited him at home and was unfolding as he arrived. One of his infant boys burned with high fever for several days, and even the doctors had given up hope. A few days later the infant died. The family mourned, cried, and wailed for the young child.

A short time later Rabbi Yitzchok Meir was again on his way to Pershischa. As he left the house, his 7-year-old son tagged along and did not want to part with him. The boy was a child prodigy, a genius who could converse with his father in Torah matters as an adult. They walked and talked without noticing that they were already at the end of the town road. The father begged his son to return home, and he continued on toward his destination. He stayed and studied with his new teacher for several weeks. Never before had he felt such depth of spirit and ecstasy as he did then.

Opposition

Many rebbes in Poland were opposed to the Pershischer and his followers. Rumors spread that they were breaking traditions, recited the morning prayers at a late hour, did not study the Torah, disrespected other tzadikim, and poked holes in miracle tales. One rumor had it that they had taken a white *gartel* (the ceremonial belt worn during prayers) that the Apter Rebbe had sent to heal an ill hasid, and dyed it black. Some even suspected that they were not fully observant Jews.

An emergency meeting was held, with more than ten great rebbes in attendance, to severely castigate, and perhaps excommunicate, the Pershischa group and warn them of their odd behavior. "How can we do this without the consent of our master and teacher, the giant among the rebbes, Rebbe Avraham Yehoshua Heschel of Apt?" objected one of them.

"That will be no problem," interrupted the Yaritchover Rebbe, a close friend of the Apter. "The Apter is marrying off his grandson, Reb Shmuel Yechiel, the son of his son-in-law Rebbe Dan of Radvil, the son of Rebbi Yitzchok of Radvil, the son of the great Rebbe Yechiel Michel of Zlotchev. The wedding will be attended by tens, perhaps hundreds, of the greatest rebbes and rabbis of the generation. We will send a special invitation to the Pershischer, he will come to the wedding, and there, in public, we will confront him with our concerns. If he admits his folly, well, then good. If not, we will propose to have him excommunicated right there in the presence of the Apter!"

The Pershischer Sends a Delegation

The Pershischer received the invitation to attend the wedding in Austilleh. Although suspecting that a confrontation was unavoidable, he prepared to leave. His highest ranking student, Reb Mendele of Kotzk, refused to let him go. He said, "I will lie down on the road in front of the coach. The rebbe will have to ride over my body to leave!" But the Pershischer was adamant, and the Kotzker said, "If you go, I go!" Knowing that most of the opposition was caused by his hasid's behavior, the Pershischer decided not to go but to send a delegation.

It was decided to send five *hasidim*: a scholar, a hasid, an intellectual, a wealthy person, and a spokesman. The scholar was the young newcomer, Reb Yitzchok Meir from Warsaw.

Over two hundred rebbes dressed in white kaftans participated in the wedding, together with tens of thousands of *hasidim.* The roads from Hiraldo to Austille, a distance of eight kilometers, were swarming with people causing a great traffic jam. Whoever did not reach Austille three days before the wedding was unable to get there.

The Pershischa delegation approached the uncle of the bride and gave him a message from their rebbe: a solution to a Talmudic question. The uncle remarked, "How wonderful. This has been bothering me for quite some time. How did the rebbe know . . . ?"

Before the *chupa* ceremony, the Apter gave a discourse raising a very difficult question from the works of Maimonides, the Rambam. From hundreds of the great minds who were near enough to hear, answers were offered, and the Apter rejected all of them.

Reb Yitzchok Meir, in a corner, mumbled a brilliant solution, but too quietly to be heard. His friends encouraged him and insisted that he raise his voice. "Now is the time!" they said. "This is what we're here for!" At the top of his voice, Reb Yitzchok Meir explained the solution. Those around him tried to debunk him. There was a commotion in that part of the room, and the Apter was told that a young scholar apparently might have an answer. The Apter asked that the young man be brought to the head table. Reb Yitzchok Meir approached and brilliantly discussed the question and its answer. The Apter did not hesitate but said, "Good, good! Go on, go on!" Everyone was craning to see the young man and to hear what the Apter was saying to him. When the young man had finished, the Apter had a very satisfied look on his face. He was beaming. He turned to the young man and asked, "Where are you from?"

"From Warsaw."

"Which rebbe do you go to?"

"The Rebbe of Pershischa."

The words hit the crowd of thousands like a thunderclap, yet no one dared to interrupt the conversation.

Later, at the meal, the Apter asked that Reb Yitzchok Meir, along with the entire delegation, be seated with him at the table. As Reb Yitzchok Meir later related, referring to himself, "There was this young man in his early twenties sitting among the sages of the generation."

The opposing camp now quickly took the opportunity. They asked for permission to speak, and Rebbe Yosef Yaritchov, a friend of the Apter, opened his talk with a caustic attack on the Pershischa, to the effect that they did not follow the Code of Jewish Law, had no respect for other rebbes, did not study Torah at all, and were late with their daily prayers. Therefore it was advised that the Pershischer and his followers be reprimanded and excommunicated. After the Yaritchover others stood up and repeated the same accusations and conclusions.

Now it was the turn of the Pershischer delegation to answer. Reb Eliezer of Grubovitz, a great and dramatic orator, stood up to answer. "Do you all have an idea of the great striving for study and spiritual development at Pershischa! It is strong and powerful. Our opposition says that we do not study the Torah?!" He pointed at Reb Yitzchok Meir. "Look here at this young man, sitting near the rebbe; he is a sample of the kind of learning we have at Pershischa!"

The Apter turned to Reb Yitzchok Meir and asked, "Yitzchok Meir, are there more of your kind of scholars at Pershischa?" Without hesitation, Yizchok Meir rose and announced in a clear voice, "There are even greater ones. I am but one of the minor scholars at Pershischa."

The opposition spoke again with sharper criticism. Suddenly, the bride's uncle rose, and all were silent. "I know Rebbe Bunim of Pershischa, a great scholar and a tzaddik."

The Apter was deep in thought and said, "The Code of Jewish Law, the *Shulchan Aruch*, is the royal road for us. Because of the exile, the road got blocked, and the Baal Shem Tov blazed new paths through the woods leading to the same destination. Now, the Pershischer *hasidim* come along and blaze trails across the wilderness? It is dangerous! We must return to the original royal path again."

Thereupon the Apter turned to Rebbe Yerachmiel from the city of Pershischa and said, "You are right there with these people; what do you say?"

Everyone was silent. Surely, Rebbe Yerachmiel, an old foe of the Pershischa, would support the opposition.

"I am witness," said he, "that my father, the holy Yehudi, may he rest in peace, used to call Rebbe Bunim 'my heartbeat' and loved him as the pupil of his eye. And he once said of him, 'I have bequeathed to Rebbe Bunim a treasure chest full of the fear of God'. And another time, when Rebbe Bunim was telling my father about his trip to Danzig, and they spoke for hours, it bothered me that Rebbe Bunim was taking up my father's time with mundane matters. I asked my father about this, and he said, 'My son, do you know that Rebbe Bunim just explained the workings of the entire universe in the spiritual realm?' And when Rebbe Bunim left, my father asked me to accompany him down the road."

Rebbe Yerachmiel sat down, and the entire throng was silent.

The opposition then put up Rebbe Shimon of Zlichov, a sage and great Torah scholar. He started again to attack the Pershischer. But in the middle of his talk, the Apter rose and said, "Stop, Rebbe Shimon! You are forever quarreling. If you were in the forest, you would quarrel with the trees!"

After that no one dared to continue the debate.

During the meal the Apter spoke again and said, "In the Sabbath prayers we say, 'And the seventh day praises and says, "A song of praise for the day of Sabbath, therefore all the creatures will praise and bless God . . . ."'' What is the connection? The answer is that when God created the world, all the creations of the six days were in great awe of Him and speechless. They were unable to praise God . . . till Shabbos came along, and she herself was a praise to God. And after the Sabbath praised God, all the creatures followed her example and praised God, too."

Later, everyone started to dance. The Apter was in the middle of a circle within circles and circles of thousands dancing and celebrating. He called Reb Yitzchok Meir, took hold of his hands, and started dancing with him. As he danced, he commented, "What I said before about Shabbos . . . applies to this young man. . . . He is Shabbos, . . . he is holy." The Apter closed his eyes and danced with Reb Yitzchok Meir as was the custom of the hasidic rebbes, a clear indication that he empathized with the delegation and would oppose any reprimand against them.

Waves of Pain

On his way home, Reb Yitzchok Meir had a premonition and hurried along. His arrival was greeted with great sadness and crying as his beloved 7-year-old son lay critically ill. He prayed fervently for the boy's recovery, but to no avail. With the best efforts of doctors, the child's condition worsened and was soon beyond recovery. He died a short time later, again on the Sabbath.

Such painful tragedies continued to visit the family. As the years went by, a total of fourteen young children of Rebbe Yitzchok Meir passed away in their infancy, while two others were married before they died. Only two survived to live on into maturity and adulthood.

Rabbi Yitzchok Meir used to tell his wife, "Be consoled, my dear wife. We will be the example for others. Whenever another person is struck by tragedy, they will look to us and say, 'Look at Yitzchok Meir and his wife; they had fourteen children who died in their infancy and they did not rant and rave against God.'"

2

A Family of Torah Giants

Once Rabbi Yitzchok Meir questioned his rebbe, "Would such tragedies happen to me if I had the proper fear of God? Is it not written that God deals with kindness with those who fear him?" His rebbe answered, "Yes, but God also promised that 'His kindness will continue to his children's children!' Your fear of God will pass on to the next generation."

The rebbe was right. Avraham Mordechai, the firstborn son of Rabbi Yitzchok Meir, was sickly and continuously suffered from pain. Yet even as a young child he showed signs of great intelligence and a kindly character. He was extremely tolerant of anything that anyone did to him and always wanted to help, someone, anyone. He never wished to anger or annoy, and he was forgiving to the extreme. It was unthinkable for him to demand any type of honor or reverence. He was blessed with a keen mind, sharp wit, and penetrating logic, and he studied Torah every minute of the day.

The great among the Torah scholars used to flock to Rabbi Yitzchok Meir's Talmud class. The lecture was unparalleled in its depth and was understood by merely a handful of those attending. Reb Avraham Mordechai sat still next to his father without a clue that he understood the lecture. After the class, however, he was more than happy to explain and answer the most difficult questions the other scholars would pose to him.

After a particularly difficult lecture, the students, puzzled and unable to understand, continued to ask. Reb Avraham Mordechai's father turned to him and said, "You also don't understand?" In response, Avraham Mordechai merely shrugged his shoulders. Thinking that even his son didn't understand, Rabbi Yitzchok Meir left the study hall. But soon the other students gathered around and asked Reb Avraham Mordechai to explain, and he did so without hesitation. Suddenly, the door opened. His father returned and was surprised to hear how clearly Reb Avraham Mordechai had understood the lecture. He turned to him and said, "Why did you give the impression that you also don't understand?" Reb Avram Mordechai said, "It seemed to me that Father didn't expect me to understand, and I didn't want to contradict Father."

At the Kotzker Rebbe

Both father and son were devoted *hasidim* of Rebbe Meirl of Kotzk, himself a student of Rebbe Bunim of Pershischa. Later the daughter of Rebbe Avraham Mordechai married the Kotzker's son.

On Friday nights the Rebbe of Kotzk would conduct his *tish*, with hundreds of *hasidim* gathered around his table singing Sabbath songs and listening to his discourses. They stood packed together, on the floor and on benches, craning to hear every word. At one particular *tish*, one of the heavy benches, packed with *hasidim*, broke and landed on Reb Avraham Mordechai's foot. The pain was excruciating, yet he uttered not a word so as not to disturb the rebbe's discourse. Luckily one of the *hasidim* noticed the pained look on his face and immediately helped to free his foot from under the bench.

The Rebbe of Izhbitze was once also a hasid of the Kotzker and had left with a group of *hasidim* and founded his own *hasidus*. He once said, "Often I am filled with yearning for Kotzk. And most of that yearning, trust me, is for the company of Rebbe Avraham Mordechai. Oh, just to see his shining face again!"

A Great Light

The Rebbe of Kuzmir once passed the small bookstore where Rebbe Avraham Mordechai worked. He asked his driver to stop, commenting, "I see a great light coming from this little shop. Who, pray tell, is the man therein?" "Oh, that is Rebbe Avraham Mordechai, the son of the *Chidushei HaRim*," he was told. The Kuzmirer left his coach, entered the store, and engaged the storekeeper in a long conversation. The others in the coach asked him why he would spend such a long time with a person so young? The Kuzmirer answered, "That young man is spiritually so mature that all of Warsaw has no idea of his great stature, and of their great fortune with such a treasure. Unfortunately," and the Kuzmirer gave a great sigh, "I don't see how he could remain in the world for too long."

The Will to Live

When Rebbe Avraham Mordechai was 30 years old, he took ill. He was weak and pale, his body racked by the pain of years of illness. His doctor was baffled and sadly said, "There is nothing I can do to help him." Others were called and left equally dejected. His father, Rebbe Yitzchok Meir, the

Chidushei HaRim, was beside himself with sadness and ur-
gency to save his great son. All his other sons had already died,
and this was the only remaining one. He did not want to leave
him for a moment. He therefore sent a letter to his close friend,
the Rebbe of Vurki, requesting that he quickly go to the Kotzker
and ask him to pray for his son. After the Vurker had spoken
to the Kotzker he immediately left to visit the patient. He was
shocked at the sight of a frail, deathly ill Rebbe Avraham
Mordechai, with ever-rising fever.

The Vurker sat down to write a letter to the Kotzker,
begging him to immediately intercede on behalf of the patient.
Many of the great tzadikim converged on Warsaw and tried
to improve the dangerous situation. The Rebbe of Radzimin
was permitted to enter the patient's room and with great
emotion whispered into his ear, "The sickness is not good and
getting worse by the minute. The doctors are at a loss what
to do. Everyone is praying for your recovery. It seems that
the very doors of heaven are closed to our prayers. There is
only one thing left to do. The patient must pray for his own
recovery. Gather some strength and beg God to help you
recover, to allow you to live a few more years so that you can
yet have a son."

His father came into the room and also begged him, "A
person must want to live. It is so written in the Torah, 'Choose
life'. If you will it, God will help you recover."

After his father had left the room, with his last bit of
strength Rebbe Avraham Mordechai sat up on the bed. He
prayed with his last breath. "Master of the world, please grant
me a few more years of life so I can yet have a baby boy. If
you grant me this, I promise to call my son Yehudah, just as
our matriarch Leah called her son Yehudah, meaning to thank
God for everything that He did. And I too, will thank God for
the miracle of healing me."

3

A Birth and a Death

And the miracle did happen. After that critical day, the patient got better. Little by little the fever dropped and the pain subsided. Soon he was on the way to normal health. The following year, 1847, Rebbe Avraham Mordechai's wife bore a son, and at his *bris* (circumcision) his father said, "I named him Yehudah Leib, as I promised on my deathbed. And he will indeed live up to the challenge of his name: he will cause the Jewish people to thank God for everything."

The Death of
Rebbe Avraham Mordechai

Little Leibeleh was an unusual child from the beginning. He was always absorbed in thought, and it was always about the world of spirit. He hardly paid attention to the games the other boys played and shunned their company. He was constantly with his father, who trained him for future leadership. One morning his father noticed that Leibeleh pushed away the bowl of grits that was placed before him. His father insisted that

Leibeleh be served grits, and only grits, for the next forty days, to teach him not to be spoiled.

Leibele loved his father. No matter if his father was testing him or reprimanding him, he always enjoyed being with him. Unfortunately this relationship did not last a lifetime. When Leibeleh was merely 8 years old, his father, the great Torah scholar, once again took ill. With superhuman patience, Rebbe Avraham Mordechai concealed the seriousness of his condition. He did not hope for a second miracle and suffered in silence. He tolerated excruciating pain, while he smiled and greeted everyone with the same warmth as always.

On the last Sabbath of his life, he prepared to attend services, accompanied by Leibeleh, his beloved son. He prayed with the same familiar fervor and devotion as always and greeted everyone with a warm "Good Shabbos!" After the meal he was in the habit of visiting his father, Rebbe Yitzchok Meir, whose fame had already spread far and wide, with hundreds joining him at his *tish* on Friday nights. But that fateful Friday evening it was already impossible for Rebbe Avraham Mordechai to leave the house. Instead he sent someone else.

At the *tish*, Rebbe Yitzchok Meir and the *hasidim* sang devotional hymns in honor of the Sabbath. He did not ask about his son's whereabouts, but unexpectedly, the rebbe asked that a solemn hymn, normally said on Yom Kippur, be sung. The words, "While his soul is still in him, He awaits the repentance of him formed from dust, to revive him and improve his end," were uttered with great devotion. No one realized how pertinent they were. Suddenly the door opened and messengers rushed in and informed the rebbe that his son was slipping from moment to moment.

The rebbe, very pained by the news, immediately left the *tish* and went directly to his room, where he lay down in his bed and covered himself as if he were asleep. Meanwhile the rebbe's wife rushed over to the home of her son and was shocked to see him so ill. She quickly rushed back to her home and directly to the rebbe's bedroom, pleading, "Do not be silent now in this terrible moment. Beg God for mercy that our son should be healed!"

The rebbe did not move but continued to pretend he was sleeping. His wife kept crying and begging, "Our son, the great tzaddik, is dangerously ill, and you are quiet?"

Finally, the rebbe answered in a weak voice, "What can I do? They have caught me on the day of Sabbath!"

His wife suddenly stopped crying and was silent.

Very early the next morning, the rebbe got off his bed and went to see his son. Hundreds of *hasidim* were there to keep vigil, and as the rebbe entered, he stopped in the doorway and stood there for several minutes without saying a word. Then he turned to one of them and asked, "How is the patient?" He was told, "The patient's condition is critical and only God can heal him."

Although it was very early, the rebbe started to recite the morning prayers. At that very moment, the patient, too, washed his face and began reciting the morning prayers. When his father had finished praying, he went into the patient's room. He heard his son reciting the blessings of the morning prayers, and he continued with superhuman strength and perseverance. Rebbe Avraham Mordechai then said the *Shma Yisroel*: "Hear, O Israel, God our Lord, God is the One and Only!" With his last bit of strength he ended with the words "God your Lord is true!" and sighed his last and died. He was merely 39 years old.

Although the tragedy was great, and all were in frightful sadness, they did not disturb the tranquility of the Sabbath and kept their tears to themselves. But as soon as the Sabbath was over, the entire city was in a fit of wrenching crying, wailing, and mourning over the loss of their beloved sage. Rebbe Yitzchok Meir, his father, cried incessantly and bitterly. When asked, "How is it that the rebbe chooses to cry over this son more than the others?" he replied, "It is not so much for the passing of my son that I cry, but for the commandment to learn with one's son, . . . he being the last one, . . . and now I can do that mitzvah no longer!"

They tried to console him: "Surely the rebbe knows that grandchildren are included in that mitzvah! The rebbe could study with Leibeleh!"

4

The Young Student

The rebbe and his wife took the orphans to their home. The Rebbetzin was no longer young, and it was not an easy job for a woman her age.

One time Leibeleh got sick, and the Rebbetzin nursed him back to health, staying up day and night. She complained about her hard work. The rebbe said, "You should be glad that you have Leibeleh to care for. Do you know the enormous reward awaiting you, both in this and the next world, for your labor of love?"

The rebbe kept Leibeleh close to himself all the time. The child ate from his bowl and slept in his bed so as not to be out of his grandfather's sight for an instant. Once when Leibeleh fell asleep on his grandfather's bed, the rebbe's assistant went to prepare the bed for the rebbe. He picked up the child to straighten him out and make room for the rebbe. The rebbe noticed and asked, "What are you doing with Leibeleh?" The man answered, "I just want to straighten him." The rebbe rebuked him and said, "Leibeleh is not crooked, and he doesn't need straightening."

Three Conditions

Thus the rebbe decided to infuse Leibeleh with his rich spiritual inheritance. He hired a teacher for his grandchild and gave him three conditions: to wake Leibeleh each day before dawn, to study with him eighteen hours a day, and to see to it that each day he composed a new interpretation of his Torah studies.

The teacher later said, "I never imagined that it would be so easy to fulfill the rebbe's conditions. But the first condition, to wake Leibeleh each morning, made me very nervous. Each day I was worried that when I walked in, the child would still be sleeping and by waking him I would also wake the rebbe. This fright finally got the better of me, and I had to quit my job after one year."

A Child Prodigy

Rebbe Yitzchok Meir would test all his grandchildren every Shabbos. Once, his little Leibele answered with brilliance. The grandfather swooped him up and showered him with kisses, saying, "I am sure that you will grow up to be a great scholar, and the light of your teachings will guide thousands."

When he was 13 years old he could recite three hundred interpretations of the first verse of the *Shma*, "Hear, O Israel, God our Lord, God is the one and only!"

His grandfather had set aside a room for his studies where he studied eighteen hours a day with his teacher. And beside that, he studied another four hours a day on his own, so that he slept only two hours a day. He was merely 9 years old at the time.

Once the rebbe from Poltosk came to visit. Rebbe Yitzchok Meir took him to Leibele's room, opened the door a crack, and whispered, "Look how my grandson studies the Torah!"

On another occasion, after a full night's study, Leibele was late to his grandfather's class that he attended each morning. Rebbe Yitzchok Meir turned to Leibele and said, "How come you got up so late?"

A boy who had stayed up and studied together with him asked, "Leibele, why didn't you tell your grandfather that you were up all night learning?!" "If I told him," replied Leibele, "I would miss his precious rebuke that sets me on the right path."

Visiting the Kotzker Rebbe

The trip to Kotzk was frightfully dangerous, but Rebbe Yitzchok Meir insisted on taking his young grandson with him. To the protests of his wife he would say, "It is all worth it if this child can but see the face of a real Jew!"

Leibele once told of how, on one of his visits to Kotsk, the silver kiddush cup was missing and one of the rebbe's secretaries thought that it was stolen because "the whole place is so open and abandoned." The Kotzker yelled at the secretary and said, "What do you mean, 'abandoned'?! It is written in the Torah, 'Thou shall not steal!'"

"That moment," said Leibele, "I felt as if there was an impenetrable wall from one end to the other end of the world that screamed, 'Thou shall not steal!'"

The Kotzker passed away when Leibele was merely 12, and Rebbe Yitzchok Meir moved to Gur, where he attracted a great following. Thousands of *hasidim* from all over Poland flocked to the rebbe. And Leibele would welcome the greatest scholars among them and ask them to teach him new Torah insights.

A Good Match

Following Leibele's Bar Mitzvah, his grandfather was eager to find an appropriate family with whom to propose a match. One day one of the older *hasidim* mentioned a very fine family. The rebbe said, "No, she will not do. For my Leibele I am looking for a daughter of a Torah scholar."

"And who may that be?" asked the hasid in surprise.

"My Yudle is just such a scholar!" answered the rebbe, referring to his nephew, the son-in-law of his brother, who both had a rabbinical family background and was himself a giant among scholars.

"I don't think that Rebbe Yudle could possibly agree to this match," retorted the hasid. "After all, he has a large family of his own and could not support another family for the rest of their lives."

As he was leaving the rebbe's room, the hasid met Rebbe Yudle and said, "I just saved you from a bundle of expenses!" and proceeded to retell the entire conversation. Rebbe Yudle was not amused. He said, "May it be my lot to have that great genius as my son-in-law!" He insisted that the hasid return to the rebbe and tell him that Rebbe Yudle agreed to the match.

"See," said the rebbe to the hasid afterward, "Rebbe Yudle is smarter than you!"

Rebbe Yudle came to the rebbe and was instructed to write to his wife and ask her if she would agree to the match. The letter was sent, and an answer arrived: "I'm already related to the rebbe, but I cannot shoulder such responsibility. It is no match!"

Rebbe Yudle returned to the rebbe with his wife's reply. The rebbe studied it for awhile, then turned to Rebbe Yudle and said, "Fine. When do we conclude the *shiduch*?"

"Whenever the rebbe is ready!"

The rebbe took a bottle of wine, and they both drank "*Lechaim!*" and decided that the wedding would take place in two years.

Rebbe Yudle returned to his town and announced the good news to his wife. He asked her to please go and visit her uncle and show that she was happy with the match by buying a gift for a few hundred rubles. She went to her uncle with the gift. When the rebbe had examined the gift, he said to his niece, "Ah, if you knew what a groom you are getting, you would have spent twice as much on your gift!"

Before the wedding the rebbe suggested that Leibele should be called Aryeh Leib instead of Yehudah Leib, so as not to have the same name as his father-in-law.

The night of the wedding the rebbe took Yudle aside and lauded the groom to him so highly that Yudle was beside himself with joy.

5

Reb Leibele and the Aleksander

After his marriage, Reb Leibele settled in Gur, where the *hasidus* was growing from day to day. Many of the rebbe's grandchildren were busy with the needs of the congregation and the individual *hasidim*. Some were even raising funds for the many social needs of the ever-increasing group. Still, the rebbe's favorite was Reb Leibele, who did not waste a second from his Torah study. At most he would be seen for a few seconds as he walked to his grandfather or to the house of study.

At the rebbe's *tish* on Friday nights, in the presence of elderly *hasidim*, the rebbe sat Reb Leibele immediately to his left. And on one occasion he called out with great passion, "Before the Messiah arrives, there will be a young man, holy and pure without a blemish, who will turn the hearts of the Jewish people to God. Perhaps he will be one of my descendants . . . ."

The Passing of the Chidushei HaRim

When Reb Leibele was 19 years old, his grandfather took ill, and after a short time he passed away on the Sabbath a few days before Pesach in the year 1867. After a massive funeral the likes of which was never seen in Poland, the elders of the *hasidim* wanted to appoint Reb Leibele as the next rebbe. He forcefully refused, insisting that he was not worthy to wear the great mantle, but agreed instead to be the Rabbi of the city of Gur. The leadership thus passed over to Rebbe Chanoch Henech, the Rebbe of Aleksander, a favorite of the grandfather.

The Aleksander was very unhappy. He went home and locked the doors while he paced back and forth, saying, "Who am I, what am I? Why do you want to choose me, the old Henech, more dead than alive? What do you need me for?"

But a large contingent of *hasidim*, with the support of the elders, kept insisting. The Aleksander saw that his refusal was futile, so he accepted the *hasidim* with great love and interest and started to pour his knowledge and fervor into them.

Yet a small group of *hasidim* still insisted that Reb Leibele be their rebbe and this caused him great aggravation.

During this tumultuous period, Reb Leibele sent a letter to a close friend, telling him of his reservation about going to the Aleksander. He knew that his grandfather respected the man but was not sure of his qualities as a rebbe. "Should I go and become his follower?"

His friend tried to persuade him to go, but Reb Leibele wrangled with the decision for nearly half a year until finally he decided to put it to a test.

When the Aleksander heard of his arrival, he invited him to dinner. After the meal, wine was brought in for the grace and the rebbe held it up, looked at it, and then glanced at Reb Leibele and said, "This wine is pure because all the dregs settled to the bottom. A Jew should also be pure with all the dregs settled to the bottom."

Reb Leibele remembered that on the last Sabbath before his grandfather passed away, the grandfather had made the identical remark to Leibele. When he had brought the wine for the grace after the meal, Rebbe Yitzchok Meir had commented, "Leibele, wine should have its dregs settled on the bottom. A Jew ought to be like that, too."

Reb Leibele decided to remain for the Sabbath and was placed next to the rebbe at the table. When the fish was served, the rebbe took some of the fish from Reb Leibele's plate and mixed it together with his own. Reb Leibele did not think he was worthy of such a great honor and at the next course ate every drop of soup. Still the rebbe took his spoon and tried to find some soup remaining in Reb Leibele's plate. Then he turned to Reb Leibele and said, "They tell of a rebbe who thought himself so important that he even ate his own leftovers." (Leftovers are usually given to the *hasidim*).

After the meal, the oldest son of the Aleksander said to him privately, "Father, how could you do this? Taking *shirayim* (the leftovers of a tzadik's meal) of a young man? Have mercy on your own honor, or else give the leadership over to him!"

"My dear son," the rebbe answered, "you can question the ways of any of the greats. But one thing: leave this young man alone. You cannot even imagine the high spiritual levels he has attained, not even a drop of them."

Reb Leibele came regularly after that, twice a year, and stayed for two weeks at a time. He would come before Rosh Hashanah and stay till after the holiday of Simchas Torah. To honor his arrival the rebbe would send his oldest son to meet him at the train station. But one year the train was late and the rebbe's son returned home, alone. The rebbe sent him again at the next scheduled arrival, and still he did not arrive. The rebbe sent him a third time, and the son said, "Why does anyone need to meet Reb Leibele at the station? He knows the way and he will get here!"

The rebbe answered, "You know very well that this young man is the promised heir of his grandfather. Now be careful to respect him!"

During the weeks that Leibeleh was with the Aleksander, he would attend the *tish* on Friday night. He would arrive when everyone was already seated, and the rebbe would seat him right next to him. The rebbe's secretary was upset about this and wondered why such a young hasid showed so little respect.

Once, to make their point, the rebbe's assistants deliberately filled all the seats so that Leibeleh would have no place to sit. But as Leibeleh walked in, the rebbe's grandson spotted him, got up, and gave him the seat right next to the rebbe.

No matter what Leibele did, the rebbe always came to his defense. Once, as Leibele arrived, the rebbe was teaching Torah. After hearing just one interpretation, Leibele quietly left the room. The rebbe overheard the *hasidim* sneering at this apparent disrespectful behavior. He said to them, "That young man is the grandson of the great sage, the *Chidushei HaRim*. He is the promised carrier of his family's tradition. None of you really understand him nor his ways. Now, be careful how you treat him."

Leibele's grandmother, who lived with him in the same house, opposed any sign of her grandson ascending to the position of rebbe. She would not tolerate someone other than her husband to lead the thousands of *hasidim*. Leibele always reassured her and told her that he was neither a rebbe nor a leader; he was a plain hasid like all the others. And his grandmother took him at his word. She insisted that he never sit at the head of the table where her husband would sit and conduct *tish*.

He journeyed regularly to Aleksander, till one day he received an urgent letter from the Aleksander telling him that he was very ill and wanted him nearby.

The Aleksander rebbe suffered for several months without once complaining or showing signs of distress. After Rosh Hashanah the rebbe's illness worsened, and for the next five months he lost strength from day to day. Finally, on Purim, he was bedridden and unable to attend services. On the last Sabbath, the rebbe stayed in bed and instructed his secretary whom to honor with being called to the Torah reading. Normally, the rebbe would be called to the Torah as the sixth person, and on that fateful Sabbath, the name announced was, "Rebbe Yehudah Aryeh Leib ben Rebbe Avraham Mordechai." It was a clear sign that the rebbe had chosen Reb Leibeleh, barely 23 years old, as his heir.

A few days later the rebbe passed away. There was deep sorrow, mourning, and rivers of tears as preparations were made for the funeral. After the seven days of mourning were over, the *hasidim* gathered to appoint Reb Leibele as the next rebbe. One very prominent hasid raised an objection: "We know that Reb Leibele is an absolute genius in matters of the revealed Torah, but is he equally familiar with Kabbalah?"

Suddenly one of them remembered a story. "Once Leibele came to the *Beis Hamidrash* and pulled a book from the bookshelf. It was a kabbalistic work, and he commented, 'I don't know what's new about this book.' Someone overheard his comment and asked him, 'What do you mean?' He said, 'One who studied the writings of Rabbi Yitzchok Luria, the Arizal, does not need this book, and if one hasn't, this book wouldn't help him.'"

When the assembled *hasidim* heard this story, they immediately agreed that Leibele was the fitting heir for his grandfather's leadership.

Many hundreds of *hasidim* had already gathered and were begging Leibeleh to accept the leadership position. With great humility and empathy he kept pushing them off and offered it instead to the older and more experienced *hasidim*. After his thousandth rejection, they asked the great sage and

tzadik, Rebbe Pinchus Eliyahu from Piltz, to speak to him and
sway his heart. Leibele complained, "Even my grandfather
wasn't asked to be rebbe till his old age, and I have to accept
such a heavy yoke when I am so young?"

The rebbe looked at him compassionately and said,
"Whatever God metes out we must accept with love, even the
pain of being a rebbe!"

6

The Gerer Rebbe

On the holiday of Shovuos following his ascension, thousands of *hasidim* came to Gur. The new rebbe, Reb Leibeleh, came to the door of the packed *Beis Hamidrash*, stood at the threshold, and said, "If I can't stop you all from coming to me, let us at least be friends."

The new rebbe refused to sit at the head of the table as was customary, and sat instead at the side. Nor did he want to wear the special clothing of the rebbes. Again, one of the elderly *hasidim* spoke to him, urging him to respect his office and the will of the people. He responded by wearing a special hat and coat in the cold winter months, while on the Sabbath and holidays he dressed the same as his *hasidim*, in an oval cap with a small brim and the plainest long jacket.

If very old *hasidim* came to him he would say, "What? Even you have come to me? Let us then learn from each other. You teach me a little, and I'll teach you a little."

The Parable of the Mountain Climber

A hasid came to the Trisker Magid and asked him, "We heard that a young man, about 23 years old, became the rebbe of the multitudes of Gur. How could that be?" The Trisker Magid answered, "It is no wonder at all, and I'll tell you a story.

A mountain climber trained for many years until he was ready to tackle one of the tallest and most difficult of mountains. He prepared his clothing and food carefully; planned his route; and dressed appropriately with spiked shoes, ropes, and pulleys. He first had to get to the mountain, a journey of several weeks. Then he set up a base camp and started his difficult climb. The higher he went, the harder it became. At times he would slip and lose a whole day's climb in one minute. Other times he had to overcome steep rocks, gaping crevices, wind, and storms. Finally, after months of agony, he was a day's climb before the summit. But a terrible depression set in, and he wondered whether the whole trip was worth the effort. He nearly gave up, but that summit kept beckoning to him, and he geared up for his last climb. The last day was sheer torture, with unbearable cold and wind. He finally pulled his worn and battered body up the last bit of rock and stood up on the summit.

Suddenly, he was shocked to see a young boy of 3 running around on the summit right near where he stood. He screamed at the boy, 'What?! This is not right. I tortured myself to get up here, and you, you little one, have the nerve to climb up here with me?!' The little boy laughed at his protest and said, 'Climb? I didn't climb. I was born up here!'

Reb Leibeleh," continued the Trisker, "was born on top of the mountain."

Hasidim

Once, the young rebbe was about to enter the *Beis Hamidrash* but heard a great commotion. He said, "I will not enter until there is quiet." An older hasid who was in his company said, "But even with your grandfather it was sometimes noisy . . . ." The rebbe answered, "Yes, it was. Except then a hasid would push himself to get a good spot. Now they are pushing the other fellow."

The rebbe once said, "There are those who come here to test the qualities of the new rebbe, while others come to meet their friends, or to hear the cantors. Very few indeed come to the rebbe."

The Little Hasid

Once, on the night of Simchas Torah, the rebbe danced within the circle of thousands of *hasidim*. Suddenly he stopped next to a very young boy, held the boy's prayer book, and recited the verses together with him. The *hasidim* wondered who that boy was who deserved the unusual attention. Later they heard the story.

The trip to Gur was often a long and difficult one, but thousands made the effort each holiday. The young boy's father was leaving for the holiday of Simchas Torah. Although his little boy begged, his father could simply not afford the fare. The boy stood by the door whimpering as he watched his father disappear toward the train station. He begged and pleaded for a few coins from his mother. She scratched together enough change for his trip to the train station. His father was shocked to see him again, and asked him what he was doing there. He said, "Daddy, I want to go with you to the rebbe."

"But, my dear child, I already told you that I cannot take you. I simply don't have the money." The boy continued to beg and cry. "No, no, my son, you must return home now. Here are a few coins to get you back home."

The boy took the few coins and went to the ticket agent and asked him for a ticket to Warsaw. The man laughed and said, "Sorry, young man. I cannot sell you anything for that!" The boy stood there with tears streaming down his cheeks. The ticket agent felt pity for him and said, "Wait, there is a way. If you get in the last car with the cows . . . ." The boy did not hesitate, ran toward the car, and climbed aboard.

As the father disembarked in Warsaw, he was shocked to see his son, muddy and dusty from head to toe. "How did you get here?" he asked. When the boy finished his story, his father cleaned him off, got a change of clothing for him, and took him along for the rest of the journey to Gur.

He was that boy.

Drafting Jews into the Army

One year the Czar decreed that everyone, without exception, over the age of 21 must join the army. Till that year, the Jewish families did not serve in the army. Religious boys knew what the army meant for them: eating nonkosher food; being unable to observe the Sabbath or holidays; socializing day and night with non-Jewish men, most of whom hated the Jewish religion; and becoming alienated from their heritage. Now, with the draft in force, they had to think of ways to avoid it.

Some forged papers to show that their age was less than 21, but soon the government caught on when not one Jew reported to the army. They changed the decree to require that all under the age of 30 must report to the army.

The police raided the Jewish neighborhood looking for draft dodgers. They arrested every young man and took him to the Czar's army. They also issued a limit on the number of Hebrew schools, and thereby many teaching jobs were lost. Then another oppressive decree followed. Jews were not permitted to wear their distinctive clothing, nor their *peyos* (side curls), with large fines for anyone daring to wear them.

The Heart of A Tartar

Then an epidemic struck the region, leaving many children sick or dying.

Once two brothers, orphans, came to the rebbe. The rebbe was leaning on his bookcase, as was his custom when receiving *hasidim*, and said hello to the boys. He leaned over a bit and said, "I, like you at your age, was an orphan. Let's be friends."

The rebbe, whose *hasidim* came to number in the many tens of thousands, listened and empathized with every tragic tale of sickness, death, bereavement, poverty and pain. He once commented to his daughter that his heart was like that of the Tartars, hard as stone and able to contain the pain of thousands without bursting.

A Demanding Schedule

The rebbe had specific hours for his *hasidim*; other than that he devoted all his time to prayer and Torah study. He did not waste a minute. He slept but two hours a night and ate sparingly and hurriedly.

He kept a very tight schedule. From six in the morning, when his assistant brought him his morning tea, he would immediately immerse himself in Torah study, then recited his morning prayers till 9:30. He would then open his door and accept the long lines of *hasidim* coming for help and advice. Each would briefly and quickly tell the rebbe his needs, listen to the rebbe's blessing and advice, and move on to make room for the next one. This continued for two hours. At 11:30 he would study Torah with his family. Then at one in the afternoon he would have a small bite to eat and again study with family members. After a short nap he returned to study Torah till the time of the afternoon prayers.

To prepare for that prayer he would speak to the young *hasidim* who came to see him. After the afternoon prayer, the rebbe was back in his room till two hours before dawn, studying Torah with great diligence. He then lay down for two hours of sleep.

The Youngest Rebbe

Although the Gerer Rebbe was the youngest rebbe in all of Poland, hundreds came to him each day to seek his blessing and advice.

As the rebbe stood to advise the thousands who came to seek his counsel, he once said, "Is it possible to give advice without knowing the four volumes of the Code of Jewish Law by heart?" He would take no longer than a few seconds to formulate his advice, answering quickly and to the point.

Once, a young hasid told him, "The evil urge keeps after me and I can't get rid of him." "When he comes," replied the rebbe immediately, "tell him to wait but a minute. Then when the minute is over, tell him to wait again, but merely a minute, and keep doing that minute by minute. After a while the evil urge will be tired of waiting and will leave you alone."

A Match Made In Heaven

A man came and told the rebbe that a match was proposed for his son. He had sent a friend to the town where the prospective bride lived to inquire about her family. "And what did he find out?" asked the rebbe. "As soon as he entered the town, he asked the first person he met about the girl's family and received a wonderful report." "In that case," said the rebbe, "the match is surely made in heaven. You can go ahead!"

The man left the rebbe's room and was suddenly hit by the strange answer. Why did the rebbe give a reason, when he usually did not? What did he mean by "it is surely made in heaven"?

He asked one of the elderly *hasidim* to please ask the rebbe about this. The rebbe answered, "A short while ago a girl's father came to see me. Because of some misunderstanding his entire village was angry with him. There was but one very close friend who still had a high regard for him. He asked whether he should move to another village so he could marry off his daughter without any problems. So when the messenger came to the girl's town and met the one and only friend of the girl's family, instead of any other person, it was clear that the match was made in heaven, and I told him to go ahead!"

Business

Another time a merchant came to the rebbe and asked him about a business deal he was about to conclude by selling iron to the army. If successful he would make a fortune. The rebbe said, "What do you need this for? Have you no other prospects?" The man heeded the rebbe's advice and declined to deal with the army. Another merchant stepped in and completed the deal. Unfortunately, the price of iron rose a great deal and the other merchant lost a fortune.

Rabbis

The rebbe was very opposed to anyone's taking a paid position as rabbi. He would rather that the *hasidim* work for a living. A man came to him after he successfully interviewed for a position as rabbi. The rebbe expressed his disapproval. The man said, "Then who will be the rabbis?" The rebbe quickly answered, "Those who won't ask me."

A rabbi had passed away and his son came to ask the rebbe for a blessing. The townspeople had offered him the rabbinate in place of his father. The rebbe disapproved. The man still insisted, and the rebbe still did not approve. Soon, the hasid went back to his town and returned the letter of appointment.

Another time a rabbi complained that the government was forcing all rabbis to be tested in Russian. "What should I do?" he asked. "Become a shoemaker!" the rebbe answered. So confident was he in the rebbe's advice, that as soon as he arrived in town he went to apprentice as a shoemaker. On his next visit he brought along a pair of shoes he had crafted for the rebbe.

America

One of the Gerer *hasidim* journeyed to America and returned some months later. Upon his return he went straight to the rebbe. "You left for America without asking advice?" the rebbe asked. "My family is poor. We had no food for the children; we were starving. I knew the rebbe wouldn't allow me to go, but I had to . . . ."

"And for hunger one is permitted to do anything? And if one has no food he is permitted to go into the fire?!" said the rebbe.

Another hasid came and asked him about going to America to seek his fortune. The rebbe took him to the window, "See the river out there? It is better you throw yourself into that river than go to that defiled land!"

The Operation

The wife of one of the *hasidim* was very ill, and he asked the rebbe's advice. He told him to take her to a specialist in

Breslau. He left without delay, and she was admitted to the hospital and operated on. A week after the operation she came down with high fever, and the doctors asked for an emergency operation to save her life.

"I must first go to ask the rebbe," the hasid pleaded with them. "You go at your own risk," they warned, "but you may not find her alive when you return."

The hasid entered the rebbe's room as soon as he arrived in Gur. The rebbe listened, smiled, and said, "Do not worry, nothing will happen to her. There is no further need to operate. And if the doctors there insist, then take her to Vienna."

The hasid quickly returned to Breslau and told the doctors what he wanted to do. They were aghast. "This patient will never make it to Vienna," they insisted. "She will certainly die on the way!"

"I will do what the rebbe told me to do," the hasid said.

"Oh, you must do what the rebbe said?" one of the doctors sneered. "Do you think the Pope makes no mistakes? The rebbe can, too."

The hasid was very offended by the remark, and it made him pack up even faster and leave. When he got to Vienna, the doctors offered him the same diagnosis: "The woman must be operated on to save her life." But the hasid would not allow her to be touched until he asked the rebbe. He came back to Gur and again cried to the rebbe about his wife's condition. The rebbe calmed him and said, "I already told you, she will get well with God's help. Do not allow an operation. Take her home and she will recover."

The hasid took his wife home and hoped for recovery. Still she did not recover. The rebbe then advised him to take her to the mineral baths. Still she did not recover.

Finally, the rebbe said, "Your painful journey is at its end. You must get a naturalist doctor and he will heal her." The naturalist doctor prescribed various herbs and vegetables, and soon enough the woman was recovering and able to stand up and walk.

The hasid, on his way home, thought of showing the doctors what the rebbe's blessing could accomplish. But he was happy enough with her recovery and went straight home. There he and his wife lived a long and fruitful life. And she would retell the story often to her children and grandchildren.

He Can See Angels

The rebbe's son said, "I am sure that my father once saw an angel." They asked him how he could be sure. He said, "Father once told me that his grandfather took him to see the Kotzker rebbe and his face was like an angel's. Father would never say anything which was not true. And if he likened him to an angel, I can be positive that he had already seen an angel."

Business

Two *hasidim* concluded a partnership and were proud to tell the rebbe about it. He said, "If you were first partners in Torah study, then your business partnership would succeed, but if not, then what is it for?"

"I am truly envious of the business people," said the rebbe, "who work all week long and wait till the Sabbath to sit and study Torah. What a joy it must be for them, a joy I yearn to have!"

The Spirit of Prophesy

The rebbe's son, Menachem Mendel, got engaged to the daughter of the Rebbe of Radomsk. Both the Gerer and the

Radomsker wanted the wedding to take place in their home town. At the engagement, the Gerer Rebbe read the engagement contract. When he came to the words, "and the wedding will, with the help of the Almighty, take place in Radomsk" he added the words, "or in Gur." By the end of that year the Radomsker passed away, and the wedding did take place in Gur.

Seeing From Afar

A young hasid came to stay with the rebbe for the holidays. One day he received an urgent letter from his wife to ask the rebbe to pray for their son, who was very ill. The hasid quickly went to the rebbe and mentioned his son's name. The rebbe said, "And what would that do?" "Please, my son is ill," the hasid pleaded. "The rebbe must pray for him!" "Why would that help?" asked the rebbe. "If the rebbe blessed my son, that would help," insisted the hasid. Finally, the rebbe said, "Why do you keep bothering me?" and with that, puzzled and confused, the hasid left. He went home and discovered the sad news of his child's death. At the moment he had stood before the rebbe the boy was no longer alive.

In the Battle Zone

One of the young *hasidim* was drafted into the army. His family tried many different ways to get him released, but it was impossible. Nine months had passed and they were beginning to give up.

His father-in-law was on his way to Warsaw on business and decided to stop in to the rebbe. He took a paper and pen and wrote seven items that he wanted the rebbe to pray for. His wife looked at the list and commented, "What? You don't even mention our son-in-law? Please, you must get the rebbe's blessing about the army." "But . . . we've tried for nine months. What else can we do?" answered her husband. "Still, how could you go to the rebbe and not mention him?" The hasid half heartedly wrote the request on the bottom of the paper.

Arriving in Warsaw, he went directly to Gur to the rebbe. The rebbe looked at the paper and suddenly said, "Yes, your son-in-law should soon be free." The hasid was puzzled. Of the seven items, the rebbe picked the least important one? He got back in line and again showed the paper to the rebbe. Again the rebbe said, " I told you already, your son-in-law will be freed!"

The hasid finished his business, left Warsaw, and was returning home through the town where the in-laws lived. He met the boy's father and told him that he had just come from the Gerer Rebbe, who said that his son was about to be freed. When the man heard this, he invited him in to drink *lechayim*, a toast to life. They sat at the table and he related the whole story with the rebbe. It was Monday.

After returning home, on Wednesday morning, he received a telegram saying that his son-in-law was free. A week later the young man was already in Warsaw and told the following story. "I was about to be sent to the front. Just before we left a doctor came to examine a group of soldiers who were previously hospitalized to see whether they were in condition to fight. Suddenly, I had this crazy idea, and I quickly joined that group. When the doctor examined me he said, "Sorry but you cannot fight. You are free to leave. I sent the telegram . . . and here I am."

Stolen Treasure

A hasid had gone to the market and was on his way home. Suddenly, one of the wagon's wheels broke and he realized that he would not be able to return home before the Sabbath. He asked the townspeople for a trustworthy man to keep his belongings till after the Sabbath. They pointed him to a wealthy businessman and assured him that all would be safe and sound in his home.

After the Sabbath the hasid immediately went to get his things. "Thank you for generously taking care of all my things," said the hasid. The rich man looked at him as though he were crazy, "Your things?" he asked, "I don't know what you are talking about!" The hasid thought that perhaps he was joking with him and asked again for his things. The man was adamant. "I don't know you, and I don't know what you are talking about!" he said. The hasid broke down and cried, but the wealthy man was unimpressed. The hasid was forced to return home without his money.

A short while passed, and the wealthy man started to lose his fortune. He decided to go to the Gerer Rebbe and ask his advice. He asked whether he should start a new business, and most importantly, what could he do about the rumor that he had stolen a fortune? The rebbe answered, "About the new business, best you ask experts. On the other hand, with regard to the rumors of the stolen money, you had better return it!"

The Bris Is Late

When the rebbe's son Nechemiah was born, he honored the Amshenover Rebbe by asking him to be the *sandek*, to hold the baby during the circumcision. The *bris* was to be in the morning, but the Amshenover hadn't arrived. They waited till noon, and still he was not there. The Gerer Rebbe sent *hasidim* to the road to see whether he was coming. The rebbe said they would wait till 3 P.M. and no longer. By 2:15 P.M. *hasidim* hurried in to tell the rebbe of the imminent arrival of the Amshenover. "I am sorry to be so late," said the Amshenover, "but I needed to redeem a Jew from prison, and I had not yet prayed the morning prayers." The Gerer Rebbe was shocked to hear this and the Amshenover added, "Oh, I know how to recite my prayers as fast as the Kotzker rebbe." And sure enough, before 3 P.M. the *bris* was already done. At the meal after the *bris* the rebbe was so elated that his face shone like that of an angel.

The Truth and Nothing But . . .

In the early days of his rabbinate, his wife had a small store to support the family. When their daughter became ill and the expenses for the medical treatment were staggering, the rebbe decided to study with several sons of wealthy families. One day, as the rebbe studied, he looked up and asked one of the boys, "Did you already recite the *mincha* prayers today?" The boy answered, "Yes!" The rebbe was about to continue studying, when he again looked at the boy and asked, "Did you say the *mincha* prayers already?" Again the boy answered, "Yes." At that, the rebbe closed the Talmud and said, "You can all go home now." And he never studied with them again.

Graf Patacki

A wealthy baron, Graf Patacki, owned the railroad between the town of Gur and the city of Warsaw. Many businesspeople, including *hasidim*, invested in the railroad. Business went badly and the Graf went bankrupt. Suddenly large sums of money were lost. One of the investors was the rebbe's son. The Graf sent a message saying that he would repay him his loan. When the rebbe's son was getting ready to go, his brother-in-law came to see him. He had also loaned money to the Graf in the sum of three thousand rubles. The brother-in-law asked if he would please take along the papers and pretend they were his. He went to see the rebbe and asked whether he could do that. "What? You are owed six thousand rubles and you are ready to lie and say that you are owed nine thousand rubles? No, it cannot be done."

The Worth of a Penny

The rebbe's son, Meir, had a very wealthy father-in-law, Leibish Berliner. The Berliners were very generous with money, both for themselves and for the poor. Even after Meir was no longer supported but had to earn his own livelihood, he continued to spend without reservation. Finally, he was in debt. He had left some money with his grandfather, the rebbe, and sent someone to ask for a hundred rubles so he could pay back his debts. The rebbe sent a message telling him when he could come to pick up the money.

When Meir, the rebbe's son, arrived, the rebbe took him to a room to show him the money. Meir was surprised to see a large chest. The rebbe opened it and showed his son a chest full of pennies. "But why . . . " asked Meir, as he tried to understand his father. "Surely you are wondering why I changed the hundred rubles into pennies for you!" said the rebbe. "Tell me," the rebbe continued, "how much do you pay a water-carrier to carry water to your upstairs apartment?" "Three pennies," answered Meir. "Yes, and how many three pennies are there in a hundred rubles?" Meir tried to answer. "Could you imagine," interrupted the rebbe, "how many years the watercarrier has to work to earn a sum as enormous as this?" Meir stood before the chest full of pennies with his head bowed and truly enlightened. That was the last time he threw around money.

The Carriage

The rebbe went for a short rest to Galicia. He went by train and then needed to ride in a horse-drawn carriage. One of the rich *hasidim* hired a luxurious carriage to take him, one that would cost thirty-five reines. The hasid told the driver not to tell the rebbe how much it cost. When the rebbe was about to board, he asked the driver, "Driver, how much is this carriage?" The driver looked at the rebbe and said, "They told me to say that it costs five reines, but it really costs much more." "In that case," said the rebbe, "you can go. All I need is a plain carriage!"

The Holy Land

The Gerer Rebbe was asked many times by leaders of movements to join in their efforts to resettle the Holy Land. He refused to join those who did not observe traditional Torah Judaism. Still his love for the Holy Land knew no bounds. And he encouraged his *hasidim* to go, on the condition that they felt capable of observing the special commandments regarding tithes totaling a fifth of the produce, and shmitah, prohibiting farming during every seventh year. Otherwise, let them stay in Poland, said the rebbe.

One time his son and a hasid were discussing the Holy Land and the rebbe overheard. The rebbe asked what the discussion was about, and they answered, "We were talking about the possibility of reviving the settlement in the Holy Land." "That will happen," said the rebbe as he turned to leave, "perhaps in thirty years. . . ." The year was 1918.

The Decree

The government had decreed that all the Jewish schools must close, and the children were to attend government schools instead. Upon inquiry it was learned that for the incredible sum of a hundred and fifty thousand rubles, the decree would be rescinded. The Rebbe of Grudzisk called for an emergency meeting. Hundreds of rabbis and rebbes came to help solve the problem. No one had any idea how such a huge sum could be raised.

The Gerer Rebbe, Reb Aryeh Leib, arrived. He asked all who accompanied the rebbes to leave the meeting. The Rebbe of Grudzisk opened the meeting and immediately proposed to raise the hundred and fifty thousand rubles. But how? The Sfas Emes asked to speak. "I will take on myself the responsibility of raising fifty thousand rubles. The Grudzisker can raise twenty-five thousand, and the Aleksander the same. The others could raise twelve thousand five hundred each, and we'll have the amount." They all agreed and thanked the Gerer Rebbe for his action. The Grudzisker invited all of them to eat. They ate and honored the Gerer with grace after the meal. He was reluctant to accept, being the youngest among them. The Grudzisker said, "The king of Israel will say grace."

The hasidim say that the time between Gerer's arrival at the meeting and the end of the meal was no longer than fifteen minutes! That is how carefully the rebbe spent his time.

More Than the World To Come

One year, there was a terrible epidemic and many children died. The government, in their effort to stem the spread of the disease, forbade burial and forced the burning of the corpses, which was against the Jewish custom. The rebbe asked that it be announced in the synagogue that whoever

buried a Jewish child would be guaranteed to merit *Olam
Habah*, the World to Come. The government had threatened
death for anyone caught burying the bodies. But one of the
hasidim, with a helper, went and stealthily did the *mitzvah*
all day long. In the evening he came to the rebbe and said,
"Today, sad to say, I buried seven children. The rebbe guaranteed that whoever buries Jewish children will get the World
to Come, but I want this world also . . . ." "What would you
request?" asked the rebbe. "I would like to be the one who
helps the rebbe don his *kittel*, the white robe, before he sits
down to the Seder on Passover night," answered the hasid.
"Granted!" said the rebbe with great satisfaction. And from
that year onward the hasid would be present on Seder night
to assist the rebbe with his *kittel*.

To the Last Ruble

A father whose son had been drafted came to the rebbe crying, "My son was drafted, his young wife is beside herself with
anguish, and my heart is torn to pieces." "Go to the town of
Rostov," said the rebbe without hesitating. "That is where your
son is stationed. Take with you a sum of rubles and you will
return with your son."

The father quickly prepared to leave and arrived in Rostov.
After a day it was clear to him that there was not much anyone
could do. He was able to communicate with his son, but there
was no way out. A few days later he heard a rumor that for a
huge sum something could be done. But who had that kind of
money? He stayed for two weeks, and still nothing. But he
trusted in the rebbe's advice and did not give up.

One day he was out on the street reading street posters.
Suddenly he heard a familiar voice. He turned and saw a non-
Jew, his best friend from his youth, who was now a high-ranking
officer in the army. The officer was elated to see him and asked

what he was doing there. He told him of all his troubles, and
the officer agreed to help. "Come to my residence in the night
and we'll talk." At night they met and the officer said, "Tell
your son to be sick with pain. His sergeant will put him in the
hospital for an exam, and there I've already spoken to the
doctors to find him unfit and release him."

The young man did as he was told, feigning sharp pains
in his abdomen. He was taken to the hospital where he was
found unfit to serve, released, and set free. On their way home
the father looked in his money bag and saw that he had spent
all the rubles for his travel and food.

The Circumcision

A hasid came to the rebbe complaining that his son was
being forced into the army, and what could he do? The rebbe
thought for a moment then said, "Your son should learn to
be a *mohel*, to perform circumcision." The father was not
happy with this strange answer and decided that before he
left he would ask the rebbe again. Again he asked, and the
rebbe said, "I already advised you. Your son should learn to
be a *mohel* and God will help him."

The young man was taken to the army and sent to a
remote part of Russia. After two weeks, an officer called the
young man and asked him to come to his office. He locked
the door behind them and said, "I am not Jewish, but my wife
is, although she doesn't observe her religion at all. A week
ago she gave birth to a son, and each night she has a night-
mare. She cries to me in the morning how her father comes
to her in her dream and warns her that if she dares not to
make a *bris* for her son, it will be the end of her! She shakes
from fright and cries. I must do it."

He now looked into the face of the young man. "I know
you are a Jew. Do you . . . know how to make a *bris*? If you

do, I will try to get you released from the army. Don't be afraid," continued the officer. "No one will know a thing."

The young man did as he was asked. A short while later he received his discharge.

On the Bare Floor

During the years of the draft, with thousands in danger, the rebbe refused to sleep in his bed and instead slept on the bare floor. He did not eat meals and snatched a bit of food a few times a day barely to keep himself alive. He said, "How could anyone eat or drink or sleep when his brethren are in danger?!"

Secret Agents

An informer told the government of the rebbe's activities. The crime of helping people dodge the draft was punishable by death, and they sent two secret agents, dressed as *hasidim*, and instructed them to wait on line at the *Beis Hamidrash* with the other *hasidim*, to see first hand what the rebbe was doing. Reb Yoel, a hasid of the Gerer and close to public officials, got wind of the plan and quickly tried to inform the rebbe. He came breathlessly to the rebbe's room and told him of the plan. The rebbe said, "They were here already!" Reb Yoel nearly fainted when he heard the words. "They were here and they found nothing," the rebbe continued. "The first came and asked, 'Shall I try to avoid the draft?' 'God forbid!' I answered. 'The Czar needs soldiers!' The second came and said, 'May I damage my body so I could free myself from the army?' I answered, 'No, no, the Jewish people are holy and no blemish may be made on them.' They left greatly disappointed."

The hasid said, "If the government is already sending secret agents, then who knows what they might do next. Please rebbe, you must stop these activities."

Poverty

The rebbe refused to take any sort of donation or salary from his *hasidim*. Even when he already had tens of thousands of *hasidim*, some of whom could support the rebbe and his family the year round, he took not one coin for himself from any one of them. Even when millionaires offered the rebbe their entire money bag on his table and said, "The rebbe should please take as much as he likes," even then he took only for others and not for himself. Instead he rented a store, and there his wife, the Rebbetzin, sat long hours and sold spices, tobacco, and cigars. He once told one of his suppliers, "If you don't want to make a profit when you sell me merchandise, that's O.K. But if you sell it to me below cost so that you lose even one penny, it will come back to you in the worst ways for you and your children." The rebbe's supplier once said, "All my accounts are handled by my accountant, except the rebbe's. His I have to do myself to be sure that I never lose money on anything I sell to him."

When *hasidim* came for the Sabbath and ate at the rebbe's *tish*, he asked each one to pay for the meals. The rebbe would go to the kitchen and figure with the Rebbetzin the cost of each ingredient to be sure that they were not making one penny in profit from the meals. The charge was the exact cost of the food on the open market.

When their daughter became ill, the Rebbetzin had to go out of town and the store was closed. There was absolutely nothing to eat. One of the aunts volunteered to help out with the children and the food. The rebbe warned her not to take anything offered by anyone. She had to go to the bakery after the Sabbath and buy up the leftover bread from the previous week. It was hardly edible even then, but by the end of the week it was hard as stone.

His Children

Rebbe Yehudah Leib Alter, the Sfas Emes, had ten children, eight sons and two daughters. Four of his sons died in their childhood. His top priority was the education of his children and he spared no effort to give them the best.

The Gift

His first son was a "gift" of his grandfather. One Chanukah, after three years of marriage, his grandfather asked him what he wanted as Chanukah *gelt*, money for the holiday. He said he did not need money, and his grandfather insisted, "But a son you do need, and so you will have a son for Chanukah *gelt*." The following year a son was born and one of the grandchildren came to tell the grandfather and said, "It's a girl! *Mazel tov!*" "Are you sure it's a girl? You're not mistaken?" The child ran to check, and of course, it was a boy. They named the boy Avraham Mordechai, after the father of Leibeleh.

Another Child Prodigy

When the child was merely 2 he could already read from the *sidur*, the prayer book. His mother wanted to continue with the study of *chumash*, the five books of Moses, but his father did not allow it. Instead the boy read the *sidur* all the time for months. Suddenly they noticed that the 2-year-old knew the prayers of the entire *sidur* by heart.

It was hard to get him a teacher who could keep up with his brilliance and thirst for knowledge. Soon he knew the entire Torah by heart, then the rest of the prophets, and on to the Talmud. His father hired the best teachers, brilliant and learned men who could satisfy his curiosity. There was an enormous library of holy books with thousands of titles on every topic of Torah. Avraham Mordechai knew every one of them and was able to speak about their contents.

Every one of the rebbe's sons was a brilliant scholar who did not waste a minute away from Torah study. They were renowned for their piety, honesty, and complete devotion to the service of God and also to their *hasidim*.

The Fire

One Friday afternoon in the spring, a fire started in one of the grain piles in the town of Gur. It grew and spread from house to wooden house. The straw roofs intensified the blaze and soon the entire town was engulfed in flame. Miraculously not one life was lost, but the devastation was awesome. The fire left one thousand people without a roof over their heads or clothing to wear or food to eat. The library of the rebbe's son, Reb Avraham Mordechai, which had tens of thousands of volumes of first-edition holy books and other rare books, also caught fire. Still, Reb Avraham Mordechai ran not to save his books but rather to his father's house to snatch up every one of his writings and save them from the flames. The rebbe's house as well as the *Beis Hamidrash*, the large prayer and study hall built by the rebbe's grandfather, the *Chidushei Ha'rim*, were also on fire. Water was too scarce to save hundreds of homes, the river too far. Soldiers came as fast as

possible, but by the time they arrived the entire Jewish neighborhood was an inferno. In order to stop the fire from spreading, the soldiers destroyed a circle of homes all around the
fire to separate the rest of the town from the flames. Their
efforts were successful. Men, women, and children walked
to the open pastures, large fields at the end of town, and
there they stayed the entire Sabbath while their homes smol-
dered and smoked. The Jews of the adjacent community
gathered wagon loads of bread and sent it to them. The sad
news spread to the towns nearby, and all came to help, with
food and clothing.

The following weeks, all over Poland, appeals for money,
food and clothing were made and help arrived from every
corner of Europe. Rebuilding started, and slowly the town was
reinhabited. When the *Beis Hamidrash* was completed the
rebbe asked that a new sign be painted and placed above the
door. His son-in-law, Reb Tzvi Hanoch, designed a beautiful
sign with the words "*Beis Hamidrash* for Torah, Prayer and
Hasidus." The rebbe asked him to erase the last word, saying, "Anyone could come here and mutter any nonsense and
say, 'Oh, I'm studying *hasidus.*' This way, either they study
Torah or pray, or they know they are in the wrong place."

Locked Out

One wicked man complained to a government official that the
new synagogue was illegal. The zoning law was that only one
synagogue was permitted per town, and since officially
Povonsk and Gur were one town, the building was illegal. The
governor decided to send soldiers, who placed a huge chain
and lock on the door. No one was able to enter.

The rebbe was pained by the new decree and sent one of his wealthy *hasidim* with contacts among government officials to see what he could do. The hasid traveled to Petersburg, the seat of the regional government, and was able to meet with one of the high-ranking officials. The official examined the papers and said, "According to this, your synagogue is illegal. The towns of Povonsk and Gur are one and the same town, and Povonsk already has a place of worship."

"Your Honor," said the hasid, "let us, with your permission, examine the books for the budget allocated for the building of the roads spanning the distance between the two towns of Povonsk and Gur."

He took out the ledgers and found the pages showing the funds and amounts spent on the road. The total was an enormous amount. The official turned to him and said, "I guess you have a point. If the two towns were one, then why is there such a long distance and a municipal road between them? I will recommend that the synagogue be reopened."

The Rebbetzin's Illness

The Rebbetzin was ill and traveled to Warsaw for medical treatment. She needed an operation in Berlin and said, "I'm not going without my oldest son." Reb Avraham Mordechai asked the rebbe for one of the rebbe's robes to take along. The rebbe gave it to him gladly, and when Reb Avraham Mordechai put his hand into the robe's pocket he felt two candles. He thought the rebbe had given them to him to light in case of his mother's death. This made him very concerned.

In Berlin the Rebbetzin was prepared for the operation by the top surgeon. Her son was in the other room reciting psalms with great fervor. When the doctor picked up the scalpel his hand trembled. He tried to calm himself but could not. Finally, he turned to the Rebbetzin and said, "I am sorry, but this never happened before. I have to excuse myself from this operation because my hand is shaking and I can't calm it down." The Rebbetzin said, "My son is outside reciting psalms. Please ask him to stop, and you will be able to continue." Reb Avraham Mordechai stopped reciting psalms. The doctor found that his hand was as calm as always and was able to complete the operation satisfactorily.

After a few weeks the Rebbetzin was well enough to return home. The doctor sent a message to the family. "We have removed a growth completely. Now if no one tells her, she will regain her health and will live many years."

The messenger, when telling this to the rebbe, repeated the last phrase and the Rebbebtzin overheard. In a short time she was again ill. She weakened from day to day, and was taken to a small town near Warsaw in the company of her son, Avraham Mordechai. She once remarked, "I have no fear of leaving this world, since I know that I have a *tzadik* like this for a son."

The Rebbetzin passed away.

The Russo-Japanese War

War broke out between Russia and Japan in 1904, and the entire army and the whole country were involved. Thousands of young and older men were sent to the front in the remotest parts of Russia. Hundreds died, and more and more were called up for battle. The rebbe's pain was unbearable as he received the news of daily casualties in Manchuria and other battlefields. He was mourning as if for his own children, and it was unbearable. When asked to eat, he would say, "How could anyone eat in this difficult time for the Jewish nation, when thousands come to me for blessings that they should merit and to be buried as a Jew, instead of dying and left on the battlefield." Hundreds of letters arrived directly from the front, telling the rebbe everything that was happening. The soldiers wrote about their superhuman efforts to observe the Torah and commandments even on the battlefield, describing how they risked their lives for prayer and Torah study, and how nothing could deter them from doing right.

The Crown Jewels of God

One young man wrote a long letter with new interpretations of Torah. The rebbe wrote back to him, "Young men like you are the jewels of God's kingdom. God prides Himself with you, because even as you are face to face with death, your heads are immersed in Torah. With young men like you, God decorates the heavens and the earth and the entire creation."

Then another draft was called. Thousands of young men had to again leave their homes for the front. Soon thousands of women whose husbands were drafted and parents whose sons were taken came to Gur to the rebbe's home and cried and wailed uncontrollably. The rebbe asked that the lamps be lit in the *Beis Hamidrash*. All gathered. The rebbe stood in his traditional place and recited psalms. He sent a delegation of ten to pray at the grave of his grandfather, the *Chidushei HaRim*. After hours of prayer, he sent everyone home saying, "Soon your sons will return."

Some days later, the war ended and the men were rerouted back toward Poland before reaching the front lines.

Sudden Illness

Although the rebbe was 57 years old, in perfect health, and stronger than most, suddenly a weakness set into him. He weakened from day to day, and with little strength he moved around, unable to do anything.

A few days before this the rebbe had just finished his great works of commentaries on the Torah.

Soon he was unable to walk, and so he rested in bed. He asked that his silver snuff box, with which he had helped heal many seriously ill people, be brought to him. The *hasidim* searched for it, but it was nowhere to be found. The most famous professors and doctors were called to help the rebbe. They were not ashamed to admit that they were totally unfamiliar with the illness and there was nothing they could do.

On the Sabbath, when his son, Reb Avraham Mordechai, came to see him, the rebbe said, "Sit on the chair," a command that his son understood to mean that he should take his place on the chair of leadership after the rebbe's passing.

Anguished Cry

All over Poland, the news brought people together in prayer, fasting, and giving charity. Still, the rebbe got weaker, and in merely eight days the end was near. At four in the morning the rebbe asked for a pan to wash his hands. He turned his head to the side and said something, and his soul ascended to heaven.

Seconds later a painful and anguished cry broke out from the thousands gathered at the rebbe's home. Telegrams were flying and every city in Poland was soon informed. From Warsaw tens of thousands were making their way to Gur by rail and wagon, and by foot. There was simply not enough room on any of the trains. Over twenty thousand people were present as the funeral procession left the rebbe's house in the afternoon. Every few minutes a train pulled in and another thousand arrived. And since the burial was far from town, hours away by foot, many thousands arrived as the procession continued.

The Sfas Emes was buried near his grandfather, the *Chidushei HaRim*, Rebbe Yitzchok Meir. At the *shiva*, Rebbe Avraham Mordechai told those who came to console him, "Father had a book of all the sicknesses, their cause, and the medicine for them. I saw the book in Father's hands many times. Now I don't notice it any more. Let us look for it; perhaps we'll find it." But as much as they tried, the book was never found.

The book of the Gerer Rebbe, who held so much holiness and love for young and old, who was a father and brother to tens of thousands, whose consoling and encouraging words gave life to the weak, recovery to the sick, and hope to the forlorn, had come to a close. The Sfas Emes had passed away.

Part II

The Sfas Emes:
His Teachings

1

Torah Is Life

Nothing

Man must never forget that without God he has no power.
And all that he does is so that God's will shall be done. And
therefore he must cleave to the Torah, the word of God that
resides in every item of creation.

God's Name

God's name is the Torah, and the entire creation is its echo.
And if we seek His name in every created thing, the light of
the Torah shines forth and lights up our life.

Form and Substance

Our physical being is material molded into form with the spirit of God. The more we realize that we are without form, desolate, and bare without the Torah's spirit, the more form we receive.

Holy Tongue

The Torah speaks to us about the world and teaches us a holy language. With it we can speak of the world in a hallowed way and discover the holy in each thing.

Deeds of Torah

The Torah penetrates the deepest depths of one's heart and infuses holiness into all of man's deeds. And when one's deeds are Torah, they are written into the Torah.

The Price Is Zero

The Torah has no price tag attached to it, and is, of course, free for anyone who wishes to study it. But to have the Torah enter one's bloodstream, to become intermingled with the Torah, to be unable to carry on a conversation without mixing in words of Torah, for that one has to be negated totally, to be absolutely a zero in one's own eyes and yearn to be filled with Torah.

A Gift and its Vessel

There are forty-eight qualities needed in order to succeed in Torah study. On the other hand, by studying Torah one acquires the forty-eight good qualities. God grants us gifts and the vessels with which to receive them.

Torah's Protection

Compared to the lofty nature of the soul, this world is dismal and dark. Compared to the Jewish people, their exile is a dungeon. Therefore they have divine gifts to help them survive and illuminate the darkness: the Torah and its commandments. These surround, educate, and protect the Jewish people in the presence of God.

Moses' Offspring

Moses taught the Torah to the Jewish people. He established pathways of wisdom and life, and those were his offspring. And although the Jewish people did not persevere to stay on his path, the *Kohanim* (priests) and the Levites did not abandon it. Thus by respecting those two lineages we are still connected to the pathways of Moses.

Preparation

After receiving the Torah, the Jewish people sojourned in the desert of Sinai for forty years. This was in preparation for spreading their teachings throughout the four corners of the globe, for making the Torah comprehensible and universal to all mankind.

Wisdom and Spirit

The Torah is full of wisdom, and that is received by each person according to his understanding. But the Torah is also God's spirit, and that is received equally by all.

A Virtual Desert

The Torah was given in the desert to teach that the world is barren, desolate, and infertile soil without it. Man has to view the world as a desert, regardless of appearance, technology, and sky-scrapers. The Torah is the organizing and civilizing force in the creation.

In the Bones

The Torah is free and accessible; all can learn and benefit from it without restraint. But to be Torah: when the Torah is absorbed in one's bones, just like an angel whose being is God's word, one needs to be like a desert, completely empty and able to receive it.

The Seal's Impression

The seal of God is the Torah. One can rise to a level where that seal is so much part of one that it leaves an impression on others too.

Oral Torah

Although the written Torah rests in the Ark and seems neglected, the Jewish people, by studying the oral Torah, delve into its precepts day and night. Just as the moon, although secondary to the sun and merely reflecting its light, has myriads of stars to console her, so too the oral Torah, a reflection of Torah light, has the millions of Jewish souls studying and enhancing its light.

Balance

Our life should be filled with a larger quantity of deeds than of learning. And even our study from day to day must be balanced by an abundance of deeds. And when one struggles to subordinate his deeds to the Torah, the Torah becomes his, and its roots anchor deep into the earth.

Inheritance

Everyone can strive to understand the Torah according to his potential. It is like a marriage: to go forth, find the right girl, and betroth her. But there is a deeper and more profound understanding of the Torah, namely that it is a legacy to the leaders of the generation. It is a gift.

Higher than High

The *Kohen Godol* (High Priest) was chosen for the role as leader of the Temple service. Still, one who recognizes his own emptiness and struggles to fill it with Torah is transformed and is even higher than the *Kohen Godol*.

Harder

The Jewish people volunteered to listen to the Torah and to observe its commandments. They soon ruined their deeds by worshiping the Golden Calf. Only their listening, their Torah study, remains in its pure form. Deeds of Torah, because they were defiled, are much harder to perform.

The Torah Sifts

The good and evil in the world do not appear as distinct entities but as a jumbled confusion. Only the Torah can help us discern the two.

Jewels

The Torah is more precious than hidden treasure, jewels, and gems. And to the degree that one values the Torah above his worldly possessions, that is how close one can come to its light.

Bones

The inner energy of the Torah is unchangeable and eternal. It is absorbed in the bones, which change at a much slower pace than the other bodily organs. Therefore it is like the tree of life and keeps one alive forever.

To See God

God created the world with loving-kindness and sustains it every instant. Yet one could live an entire lifetime and never have seen God in his daily life. Only the Torah can guide us and help us to recognize God's deeds in nature and thus to find God.

Like a Tree

The Torah is like a tree. The spreading branches are the Torah's light spreading into one's life. The more they spread, the stronger and firmer become the roots of the Torah and thus give forth more light.

Blind

A blind person would rather find his own way without the help of one with eyes. So too, each one has to light his own lamp, do his own good deeds. The light of the Torah, however, is not his doing at all; it is totally a gift from God.

Drowning

One who is drowning in water is told to hold tightly the rope thrown to him by rescuers. The Torah is the tree, the rope, of life. And by holding it tenaciously, one is worthy to be saved by it.

Letters of Light

The essence of the Torah is God's pure light shining to us through its Hebrew letters. They are spread through the universe, and the Jewish people are assigned to find them. The *mitzvos* help make them manifest.

Working

There is the written Torah given by God from heaven, like the mana that fed the Israelites in the desert, and the oral Torah that man has to work for, like the land of Israel, which they had to farm.

Embarrassing

The ancient, voluminous and awesome wisdom of the Torah follows the Jewish people wherever they wander in exile. And when we ignore our great heritage and instead pursue other pastimes, what an embarrassment that is for our Torah!

Wasted

God gave you wondrous senses, talent, logic, and intelligence to serve Him and study His Torah. And what are you using them for?

Merit

When the Jewish people live by God's word, they merit to understand it more and more.

Yisroel

The Israelites' name, Yisroel, is the permanent state of holiness they enjoy. But even when they are wandering, and in a temporary place, the Torah and its holiness travel with them. They are never without it.

Fragments

The original Ten Commandments on stone tablets might have publicly spread the word of God throughout the world. But because they sinned, the Israelites could teach the Torah only in more subtle ways. Still, the fragments of the original Tablets were always with them in the Ark of the Covenant. And throughout history they search for those fragments, to reconstruct the original and totally public Torah.

Wholeness

Every part of the human body serves a function together with the rest. All of them interact, communicate, and enhance each other's well-being as one whole. The Torah's commandments, too, although we may not understand them, are all parts of a spiritual whole we all need. And it is their wholeness that purifies everything that comes in contact with them.

Absorbed

There are two aspects of the Torah: one is to receive the Torah, and then the Torah is absorbed into the bloodstream and bones. The learner becomes a Torah personality and leads a life of Torah.

Diligence

Each person has Torah in the deepest depth of his heart, and through great diligence and study it is uncovered.

Among the Nations

There is the written Torah, observed and followed when the people study it. But what of the times that the Jewish people are among the nations? They then follow the Torah as an inherited trait; it is their bones and blood.

Torah's Essence

The essence of the Torah is higher than its words. It is beyond the human realm and out of the reach of angels. Our forefathers, giants of faith, struggled to bring from heaven a Torah with words, sentences, and paragraphs so that their descendants could understand it.

Stone Against Stone

There is always a stone on the well. God created the evil inclination, a stone blocking man's every good deed. The Torah is also a stone and eliminates the other stone. And if not, then the Torah is water and dissolves the stone.

Digging Deep

There is the Torah that descends from heaven, and the Torah that one digs deep for and in the end is given to him as a gift.

Torah's Decrees

Although now we may not understand the meaning of all the Torah's decrees, someday we will. All will be revealed, and all will understand.

Faith of Man

There is truth coming from heaven, and it is the written Law. And there is faith, the part that man adds.

Hidden Pathways

There is the essence of the Torah, and there are the pathways of the Torah. Those are hidden, like forest trails covered by leaves. The trailblazers know about them, but to others it is a total mystery how one finds his way. There are such paths in our everyday life, and those fortunate enough to find them can be led to the essence of the Torah.

Share of Light

The essence of the Torah is a heavenly light far removed from the world of our experience. Yet every Jew has a share in that light and is able to connect his ordinary earthly life to the Torah.

The Torah of Man

One can learn God's will from everything that happens. And because we must strive to do every deed according to the Torah, it is called the Torah of Man, the guide for daily living.

All True

The Torah is truth, *emes*, the first, the middle, and the last letters in the Hebrew alphabet. It is true from the beginning to the end, together with its numerical equivalents and the combinations of any of its words, verses, chapters, and sections of each of its five books. They are all true.

Gate to the Treasury

The Torah is a gate to enter and attain the fear of God. And the fear of God itself is a treasury for the Torah.

All Directions

The world was created with a *beis*, the second letter of the Hebrew alphabet, closed on all sides except one in order to look in no other direction but foreward and to know God by looking in the direction of the creation. On the other hand, the Ten Commandments start with an *aleph*, the first letter of the Hebrew alphabet, pointing in all directions and completely open. With Torah we can know God without contemplating nature.

Water and Fire

The Torah is both water and fire. Water descends to the lowest place, the body, to quench the body's thirst for the divine. Then it raises the body like fire that rises to the heavens.

Renewed Torah

The Torah is not an inheritance, and the Torah you knew yesterday is not the same as the one you need to learn today. Therefore each day one must prepare vessels for the new Torah he is receiving.

Drop of Water

Familiarity cools original deep love. The love for the Torah, on the other hand, increases from day to day. And each letter is beloved by her students as fish crave every new drop of water.

Quickening the Dead

Every letter in the Torah has the power to quicken the dead, if only we knew how.

Means of Help

The Jewish people can seek, investigate, and even try every other means of help, but they will never be helped completely except through the power of the Torah.

Immersed in Torah

Man is made in the image of God that is concealed inside him. When he connects to the Torah and immerses himself in it completely, he becomes Torah through and through.

Accepting Her Ways

The Torah is comprised of laws, exactitude, and judgments and may be perceived as without kindness. Those who accept her ways, however, find her true nature of love and kindness.

Repeated Message

Each person received from Mount Sinai the message he must repeat in his lifetime.

Torah Scroll

With the good deeds that he does, man writes his own Torah scroll. And that scroll is open for all his descendants to see, study, and emulate.

Inner Completion

There is divine satisfaction with the creation, and it is the Torah. It is the inner completion and wholesomeness found in the world.

One Command

Just as the world was created with one command, while the details were worked out later, similarly, the entire Torah is in one commandment, and the details are in the rest of them.

On Every Level

The Torah exists on every level, in all times, spheres, and places. And whether one is on the highest or the lowest level, there is the Torah just for him.

Even If Only One

God speaks the words of Torah to each individual. Thus even if there is only one person who listens to her words, the Torah will have a place in the world and grow from there.

Inside and Outside

The eye and the ear are two vessels that receive the wisdom of the Torah, and both are needed. The eye receives light rays just the way they are, while sound waves change inside the ear. On the other hand, sound is experienced inside the body, while the experience of sight is merely on the outside.

Nature and Torah

Nature itself is in harmony with the Torah, and man should find nothing contradictory in it.

Tongue of Truth

The Torah gives life and freedom to all created beings and makes the tongue speak truth.

Planted

The Torah is infinite and surely no one can receive its entirety. Yet it is planted into one's heart in the way it is received, studied, and observed.

Tributaries

Just as water flows from the river to the tributaries, so too the wisdom of the Torah flows from it to the other languages and nations.

Torah of the Earth

The written Torah is heavenly, while the oral Torah is of the earth; they are two sides of the same coin. The higher one climbs toward the spiritual levels of the Torah, the lower and the more earthly the influence of his Torah becomes.

Tiny Spark

The written Torah is etched into every Jewish heart and is the Tree of Life. What can man do? Even if he seeks its knowledge day and night, what does this amount to? It does accomplish something though; the tiny spark opens and grows till it fills his life with its holiness.

Torah Lived

The written Torah is received with far less preparation than the oral Torah, which is nothing less than the Torah lived.

Colorful Detail

The Torah has a theme, direction, and focus, and man's life with all its colorful details should be a reflection of it.

Torah Connects

One can speak many tongues, yet all his talk may amount to nothing. But with the tongue-healing Torah, his words connect to God's holiness, are full of sense, and bring healing and peace.

Primary

Everything one does must be connected to the Torah. Then the Torah is his primary concern, while work is the secondary concern.

By Doing

It is never possible to understand God's commandments. By doing them, over and over, we start to understand them.

Wiser Body

Torah study and observing God's commandments change not only one's spiritual being, but even his physical being. He becomes totally wise; not even his body remains foolish.

In the Words

The Jewish people, at Mount Sinai, accepted the Torah with total sacrifice. That acceptance is inscribed in the words of the Torah. And whoever studies it diligently will experience that awesome event as if he were there.

Expanding the Mind

How is it possible for a creature to be a witness that God is Lord, King of the universe? It is only because his witnessing is truth, and the truth causes an expansion of his mind with greater understanding and intelligence.

Lord of Nature

When God declared His kingdom on Mount Sinai: "I am God your Lord," every creature thought that He was speaking to him. When they heard, "who has taken you out of Egypt," they knew that He was speaking to the Jewish people. Still, the Ten Commandments were an address to all of nature. And God declared that He is the Lord over nature and none of it can contradict the Torah.

Liver, Heart, and Brain

There is the liver, the heart, and the brain. The life-giving forces travel higher and higher, from the liver to the heart, and from the heart to the brain. The outer husk of food is the lowest level, nearly all material. The next level is a mixture of good and evil, and the highest is to connect to the spirit within. With the help of the Torah, one can derive the spirit from food that goes directly to his brain, and from there to the heart and then to the liver.

In Your Heart

The Ten Commandments resonate in the hearts of the Jewish people forever. Their sound recedes into the background, however, unless stimulated. By observing the commandments first, we get to hear the voice of God from the depth of our hearts.

Heart and Soul

The Torah and its commandments can be understood in endless layers of higher and higher spirituality. And no matter whether one's connection is to the loftiest of intentions or to the barest, minimum observance: if done with heart and soul, it will bring blessing and reward.

Roadsigns

The Torah is the guide, like roadsigns pointing the way. If you are already on that road, the road of blessing, it points the direction toward your destination. And even on the roads leading to nowhere, the road of curse, the Torah has signs showing how you can return to the right road.

Torah for All

The Torah is full of commandments, advice, prescriptions, and parables to guide and point the way. No matter what one has done in the past, whether good or evil, even if he is wicked, the Torah does not cease to speak to him. If he is a thief, or even a murderer, the Torah's laws include him. No one can say, "I am too wicked for the Torah!" After all, there are laws in the Torah even about the most wicked. And knowing that, no one should feel alienated, but should open the Torah and find the advice pertaining to his life.

Purify

The purpose of the Torah and the commandments is to purify those who observe them. And with that they will be able to absorb even more light and holiness, preparing them for the ultimate encounter with the Creator. In the World to Come their souls will be rewarded with the purest light of those deeds.

Beyond the Human

The laws and judgments of the Torah are divine, far beyond human understanding. Its civilizing properties are way ahead of its time and just beginning to be understood by the rest of mankind.

No Fear

The Torah is the voice of Jacob, the strength of the Jewish people. And one who connects to it need not fear the hands of Esau, the wicked one.

Bonding

Although nature is full of wonders and awesome wisdom, it has boundaries and limitations. The Torah, on the other hand, is infinite, and whoever bonds with it goes beyond the natural.

Equality

A judge ought to consider the guilt and innocence equally without leaning or prejudice.

As a Gift

After Moses toiled to understand the Torah, for forty days and forty nights, it was given to him as a gift. Similarly, when man toils to leave the material world behind, the World to Come is given to him as a gift.

Key to the Door

We are faced with two doors. The first is entry to fear of God and the second is entry to the Torah. Actually, we have the key only to the first door, while God has the key to the inside door. God counts the number of steps you have taken once you enter the first door. Then he opens the second door the same amount.

The Sages

Where is the Torah? It is in the life of the sages of Israel who contain it. On the other hand, if all of Israel united their energies, they would also receive the full measure of the Torah. Similarly, every individual, in the measure that he is ready to risk everything for the Torah, and to the extent that he unites with his brethren, receives the fullness of the Torah.

Learning to Swim

The Torah is compared to water. Those who study on a simple level wade in up to their ankles, their belly, or their necks. But there is a deeper understanding that is like deep water without end. There, only expert swimmers can enter, lest they get washed away, never to return. How can one swim there? Only he who totally negates his being and offers no resistance, who becomes weightless and light as a feather to be carried by the water, can do so. But who will teach him to swim there? One cannot learn to swim on dry land. He must enter the water. Thus one must start learning, throw himself and immerse himself totally into the Torah. The Torah itself will teach him how to swim in its life-giving waters.

Royal Garments

A prince asked his father, the King, to appoint him a ruler in one of the provinces. His father said, "Don my royal garment and wear my crown, and everyone will know you are my son." Similarly, when we study the Torah, we find God's garments, the documents declaring God the creator and King of the universe. By delving into the Torah, we weave the divine garments for our soul, whose light also illuminates our physical being in our lifetime.

We Can

We should not think that it is impossible to fathom the Torah, nor should we think that we cannot have the light of the Torah forever.

It Is Up to You

Man can choose to be close to the Torah: it is there, merely a breath away from his reach. And by his effort he bridges the gap, and it is in his heart, mind, and actions.

Heaven and Heart

There are two blessings for the Torah, one before and one after reading it. The first is to connect the Torah to its roots in heaven, and the second is to connect it to our inner heart of hearts. There it will remedy all the past actions, speech, and thoughts.

Enthused

The Torah was given in the written and the oral form. The written Torah is etched into the heart of each Jew, and the oral one is our ability to verbalize and become enthused with the power of the Torah.

Open and Close

No other creature besides the Jewish people can open the text of the Torah and interpret it. And each individual has a share in the Torah that no one else has. Just as each of the ancient rabbis interpreted, opened his Torah discourses in a different way, so too, on a lesser scale, each and every Jew can open a discourse to explain the Torah. The Torah was not given only to heavenly types, but even to the plainest Jew.

Just as it is important to open and speak words of Torah, so too it is important to close and protect them, watch them carefully lest they go to waste. After all, the entire Torah, its study and observance, is intended to bring one to the fear of God.

Threefold Torah

The Torah is in thought, speech, and action. In thought: to be filled with so much enthusiasm that it overflows into another's heart. In speech: words that emanate from the heart enter the heart. In action: to find the light of the Torah in all things.

Those three will make our entire life Torah, so that we shall have wisdom and understanding, fear and love of God, completing them with action by observing the commandments.

The Bridge

God, the Torah, and the Jewish people are all one. The Torah is the bridge between God and the Jewish people; it connects the lowest with the highest, and they need to be connected. One who is devoted to the Torah can find in it secrets as high as the heavens and as deep as the sea, hidden from all other creatures.

Stone to Stone

The Torah was given in two forms: written and oral. The written Law is etched into every Jewish heart, the deepest depths, the "heart of the wise man," and is on his right side. When the Israelites heard the first words of the Ten Commandments, the tablets of stone pushed aside the foolish heart of stone on the left side. At that moment they had only one heart. Had they not sinned, they would have remained with their one heart. Even so, it is now easier to push aside the "heart of the fool" with the power of Torah. And that power is reawakened when we diligently study it and express it verbally, and it becomes the oral law.

Reward

The commandments of the Torah are different from those of a king. A human command is but words, while the word of God is an opportunity to unite with His power. Therefore the reward for observing a *mitzvah* is the *mitzvah* itself. It connects you to the divine power within it. That is why the Israelites at Mount Sinai said, "We will do and we will listen," because they realized that once they do, the commandments will give them the energy to understand.

Torah Equals 611

The word *Torah* has the numerical equivalent of 611. Add to that sum two words, fear and love (of God), and it totals 613, the number of commandments in the Torah. Fear and love of God are the roots of all the commandments, corresponding to the first two of the Ten Commandments: "I am God your Lord" (love of God) and "Do not have other gods before Me" (fear of God).

We know how to fear the awesome God, king of the universe. But how do we get to love Him? That is a gift granted by God Himself. Thus there are 611 commandments acquired by our own choice + 1, the fear of God, similarly acquired. The total is 612, numerically equal to *bris*. This is the covenant that God shares with the Torah and the Torah shares with the Jewish nation. It is a covenant shared with past and future generations, just as God exists in the past and the future as well as in the present. And by participating in the *bris*, we connect to the generations of all time.

It Is There

The Torah is found in all places and all times, and is revealed only to the Jewish people. All are blind till God helps them see. Therefore, even after we have sinned and been exiled, if we repent, God reveals and helps us see that the very place where He stands at that moment, there Torah is found.

Beyond

The Torah is on the highest spiritual level, beyond the material world. What we received is the ability to live our life according to the Torah, thereby uncovering its hidden light. By beaming its light into our deeds, we find its light in all things.

The Call of Torah

A voice came forth from Mount Sinai that even now is as powerful in its call as then. While nations can read the details of the Torah's message, its call is exclusive to the Jewish people.

Without Number

The letters and words of the Torah are physical and have a number. The inner truth of the Torah, its roots and energy, are spiritual, without number and infinite. Similarly, man's abilities have a number and are limited, but their roots are in the soul, which is infinite.

Root Purpose

Just as the angels have a clear knowledge of the root purpose of their mission, so too every individual can attain that knowledge by connecting with the Torah.

Balanced

The two thousand years when the world was desolate without the Torah were balanced when the Jewish people stood in the desolate desert before Mount Sinai and received the Torah.

Highest Light

Torah's light is spiritually so high that it would be impossible to discern without the commandments. The soul of man, too, would be impossible to connect with if not for the vitality it provides for the body's movements.

Holding the Rope

If someone is drowning, the more tightly he holds the rope, the better his chances of survival. Similarly, the more tightly one holds the Torah, the Tree of Life, the more life it gives him.

Not to Stray

To understand the Torah we need a raising of our conscious-
ness. All that, however, is in the realm of the soul. How
do we get the body to participate in the Torah and observe
mitzvos? By allowing our soul to be the master over our body,
drawing it into the service of God and not letting it stray to
the right or the left.

Happy to Do

By yearning all day to observe the commandments, we get to
do them. We inject this yearning into the blessing before we
observe a *mitzvah*. It contains the love and joy we feel about
the *mitzvah*, which never leaves us. Thus we have the *mitzvah*
both before and after we do it. We are happy that we are about
to do it, happy that we are doing it, and happy that we did it.

A Master

The Oral Law is called Torah *shbaalpeh*, the Torah of the
mouth. It also means the Torah of one who is *baal*, a master,
over his mouth. Since he guards the breath of his innards, he
is worthy to understand the oral law transmitted mouth to
mouth, breath to breath.

Loving Calls

The entire Torah consists of names of God in various combinations. Those who study it, expound it, delve into its details and wisdom are all calling God's name. And the more often His name is called, the more intimate the caller gets with Him, and God responds in kind.

Torah and Prayer

Torah means guidance on the path of life, on the path of movement. Prayer, on the other hand, is being still and standing before God. Torah is getting there while prayer is being there. And although prayer is on a lower spiritual level compared to Torah, it is the foundation for Torah.

Torah is in one's mouth and moving out to others, while prayer is still in one's heart and is the foundation.

Heartbeat

God's desire is that His covenant with you should not have to be reawakened and caused to be remembered. It should be part of you, like your breath and heartbeat. When you observe the Torah you should do "by not doing."

Even in Heaven

If one desires the Torah so much that even if it were in Heaven he would climb to get it, it will not be far from him. For him who tries, it is near, and if not, it is far.

2

Soul's Energy

True Caring

The garments, the physical part of each person, are separate and different from those of all others. Yet all of their inner spirits are similar and united. And with the Torah, an inheritance of pure spirit, all individuals can find unity. And when they do, they see no difference between caring and loving for their own life or the life of any of the others.

Gathered and Infinite

When individual numbers are dispersed, they are finite and limited. When they are gathered together and become a collective, a singularity, they are infinite and without number.

Collective Mind

Abraham abandoned the idol worship of his family and realized through logic, deduction, and analysis that God is the
master of the universe. His descendants each have some aspect of his mind, each with a different flavor and degree, no
two alike. And so the conception of God varies from mind to
mind, from individual to individual, together comprising the
collective mind of the Jewish people.

Why We Are

The ultimate question for man at birth and death is: why was
I created? And really the world is too dark, and spirituality too
concealed, to find the answer. Only with the light of the Torah
can we ever hope to know the root of our soul and why we
exist.

Utterly Alone

In order to mature spiritually, man needs to feel that if not for
God, Who is his total redeemer, he remains alone and isolated.

The Body Too

God has mercy on our heavenly soul, and, after all, even our
body is His work.

Silence

While the inanimate, vegetative, and animal energies in man are a mixture of good and evil, his divine breath of life is always pure. It is there to help him sort out the good from the evil. And therefore he needs to protect it with silence.

Soul of Man

The soul of man is the root of Torah's light.

Food

When man subordinates his body to his spirit, he is sustained by the spirit within food. Each person, according to his level, is sustained by a different amount of spirit.

The Cloak

The soul is surrounded by a supernal garment, although the physical body separates between them. After the body dies, the supernal garment wraps the soul. All our life we yearn for that cloak and can attain it by observing the commandments.

He and He Alone

The completion and wholeness of a human being lies in reaching the place and purpose for which he, and he alone, was created. And that is nearly impossible without the help of God.

Purity

Standing before God at Mount Sinai was the single most awesome experience for the Jewish people and for each individual soul for all time. It completely and totally purified all souls forever. Now, if one comes to purify, he merely returns to that pure state of yore.

How Is It?

It is wondrous indeed that a spiritual soul is able to stay inside a physical body. One needs always to focus on the divine, and then his body can remain a vessel for the soul.

Intelligence

The soul's union with the physical brain results in intelligence. That intelligence is in danger as it flows through the nervous system to activate the muscles. It can degenerate to the level of the physical, or it can raise the physical to its spiritual level.

All Come to Man

Earth is the substance from which everything originates, and everything returns to it and decomposes. Man, made from the earth's dust, is the foundation of everything in the universe, and to him, too, everything returns. Whether he meets the other in his thought, speech, or action, all things come to him to be raised up and reach perfection.

A Needle's Eye

The spiritual world, where all blessing resides, is above and separate from the material world. What is needed is a channel through which the blessings can descend. And because spirit is infinite, without limit or size, even if the channel is as tiny as the needle's eye, it is enough.

You Can Do It

Man's soul descends from the upper to the lower world and is in a state of inferiority. He must not feel that he is inferior and low, however. He must lift himself up heavenward and compare his sorry state to the glory of God. And by doing that he realizes that God, the all-powerful, created him and he can therefore accomplish all that is required of him.

God's Seal

God's seal, inscribed in every soul, must be guarded with one's life lest it get shrouded with evil and wickedness. And the more it is protected, the more it shines its light into our heart and life.

Immersed in Light

Receiving the good is different from being immersed in it. A tree has leaves, bark, a trunk, and roots. While some connect to a part of the tree, others connect to the tree itself. A well has standing water, but a brook, a fountainhead, has fresh water constantly bubbling forth from it. Similarly, every soul has light and wisdom. But to be immersed in light and wisdom, that is something else!

Accomplished

Each human being has a specific task to accomplish during his lifetime. As soon as his mission is accomplished, he leaves the world.

God Particle

There is a God particle in each being from which he can draw all his strength. His task is to connect all his activities to that particle.

Time and Place

Every human being has a place and time and so does every soul. The souls of the spiritually developed are connected to all others, and thus they are in all places and times.

Deep

There are spiritual realms on the surface, and others deep inside the natural world. The souls of some connect to the surface, those of others to the deep.

No Two Alike

Every instant has its mission, exactly what is supposed to happen just then. No two moments are alike. Similarly, every place and every soul, all have their assigned destiny. Yet, despite apparent differences, God the creator sends His light to all of them and unites them in peace.

In Tune

The more in tune the body is with the soul, the more the soul lights its way. And the more the Jewish people attract the nations to their way, the more the Torah lights their way.

Familiar

Souls are from the highest sphere and are familiar with God. Yet, in the present state, in the material world, they are estranged from Him. And when their souls are stirred, as at Mount Sinai, they again experience that familiarity.

Body and Soul

The body and the soul are at odds with each other as much as a farmer boy who married the princess. All the delights he can offer her are nothing compared to her royal origins. Those who study Torah and perform physical commandments create harmony between their body and their soul.

Soul's Memory

Every soul was present at Mount Sinai as God spoke the Ten Commandments, and that memory is part of its being forever.

The Giver of Life

When God created man, He breathed into him a spirit of life. Similarly, when the time comes to quicken the dead, everyone will first die, then live. At Mount Sinai, too, with each word their souls flew out of them, and with the next word they returned. They were being raised level by level and might have reached the level of angels.

Signs

Some of the commandments are called signs: they must leave their mark on us, change us, and make us better.

Finding Light

Every item of creation contains in its deepest depths a spark of supernal light. That is the blessing. And we can, by ignoring the packaging, the shell, seek and find that light. And when we do, we realize that we have the power to turn darkness, the curse, to blessing and light.

The Oral Law

Man possesses a holy spark within him, tiny, yet all-powerful. And he needs to allow the spark to spread and illuminate the lives of others. But once the light starts to spread, all of it may be lost. Therefore it needs boundaries: that is the oral Law. And even with those boundaries he needs stronger ones and more of them.

Dead or Alive

The soul of man lives forever, while the physical body dies. The wicked are therefore called dead, because they indulge purely in the interests of the body, while the righteous are alive with the purposes of the soul.

One needs to be mindful not to allow his attention to the body to block his eyes from seeing his soul.

Where to Look

Where does one need to investigate and look again and again?
Where truth is not apparent: the place of deceit and falsehood,
the material world. And what are we looking for? We seek
the hidden kernel of spirit and truth, placed by God into every
item of creation.

Brothers in Sin

The Jewish people are all connected in their souls and are all
one. And thus if one sees another committing an improper
act, he must ask himself why he has seen it. He needs to repent for some such act and cause the sinner to repent, too.

Lifting

At Mount Sinai the Israelites learned about the world of the
soul. In the Land of Israel they learned about the body, how
to lift it to the level of the soul.

Connections

The soul of man waits in its heavenly home for a bridge to
connect it with the body and illuminate it with light. If man
studies Torah and observes the commandments, the connection is made, and the body is infused with a brilliant light.

Backward and Forward

The repentant not only saves himself, but by purifying his soul also saves the future generations attached to his soul. Thus his repentance goes backwards, to rectify his erring ways, and forward, to straighten the road to the future for his children and generations to come.

3

Humble Spirit

Whose Honor

One ought to minimize the attention and honor resulting from his achievements. Rather, he should be humbled to the very earth, so that all honor is directed to God, Who gives to each the energy to accomplish. Thus the kingdom of God is revealed.

Desert

Because we have free will it is difficult not to assert our independence and to feel our power. Still, only if we humble ourselves as a desert, helpless and empty, can we receive the word of God.

Man's Humility

The honor received by a human being will never diminish God's honor. But the more one makes nothing of himself, the more honor accrues to God. Even the Torah scholar, who is humble and makes nothing of his accomplishments, should not worry that God's honor will thus be diminished. For the opposite is true.

Man the Desert

There are four levels: the inanimate, the vegetative, the animal, and the communicator or human being. The communicator is called a *medaber* and is the highest form in creation. But he is nothing and nobody on his own, unless he makes himself a *midbar* (another reading of the word *medaber*), a desert, empty and desolate without God.

True Wisdom

To completely subordinate oneself to the Creator is true wisdom. One then realizes that he is connected to the root of all being. That is the wonder and amazement of the material world: although material, it is also partly spiritual.

Who Is Blessed

It seems as if the *kohanim* (priests) are the highest because they were chosen to channel blessings unto others. Yet, on the spiritual plane, the plain folk precede even them. They are the ones who are blessed.

Future in the Past

For God the past and the future are on the same plane. He knows that with His closeness we all return to Him. Therefore He shows His closeness even before we repent. In addition, whenever God is good to the Jewish people they humble themselves, and even more so if they do not deserve it. And therefore they really deserve it, because they do humble themselves.

Merely Dust

Man must negate himself totally to God his creator. He has absolutely no life of any sort without Him. And he ought to consider himself as the dust from which he was formed; without God that is what he would be.

In the Dust

Everything grows from the earth, from dust. In order to survive you must have a place in that dust, so as to be like the dust of the earth. Do you?

Earth

One who makes nothing of his accomplishments, just like the dust of the earth, becomes like the earth, the foundation of all.

Always the Same

Although one sees that his *mitzvah* brought light to the world, or that his kindness helped another beyond words, he must not change. One must not allow his own deeds to affect him and must not become impressed with himself. He must continue to think of himself as the selfsame person as before.

Reward

The reward of one who does not change just because of his great deeds is that God will shower him with blessings, too, without his having to change.

Full Glory

If one is not ashamed of his efforts and deeds, he will deserve to see that God's kingdom, revealed through His deeds, is there in its full glory.

Triviality

It is because man realizes the insignificance of his deeds that God accepts them.

Man's Shame

One who is ashamed of his puny deeds and meager Torah study will not have to be ashamed of his studies when he reaches the heavenly World of Truth. Otherwise, who needs the numerous holy books he has studied? Does God need them in His heavenly abode? It is only the shame, man's negating himself totally before God, which amounts to anything.

Creativity

When anything is born, be it a baby or the product of creative activity, its creator must first lower himself as nothing before God.

Micro-Concepts

You can be humble before God without any understanding, because you know that you are an insignificant speck before His greatness. And even if you happen to be inspired, and filled with awareness, you also realize that your concept is dwarfed by the awesome mind of the Creator.

Lowest Point

We all need to acquire three good habits: to be generous, to be humble, and not to indulge in physical passion for its own sake. One must be humble: the Torah seeks only the lowest to come and dwell there.

True Humility

The wicked say, "I am really too important to humble myself, but before God I will make an exception," whereas the righteous wonder how it is possible for a creature to feel any sort of importance in God's presence.

Smaller and Smaller

All true understanding leads to humility. The more one understands, the deeper his probing, grasp, and comprehension, the more humble he becomes, feeling smaller and smaller compared to Him Who understands everything.

Spiritual Cycle

There is a spiritual cycle moving up and down. He who lowers himself is given the Torah as a gift. But when he receives it, he becomes conceited and again must be lowered, to be raised again in turn.

Without God Nothing

There is no true worship of God without complete humility. That is a prerequisite of any godly act and is the basis of repentance. If man recognized that without God he has no life in which to choose right or wrong, could he ever do wrong? After all, God is pumping his heart and sending the messages through his nervous system!

No Space

The world of the spirit does not take up space or time. Therefore the Jewish people can be the highest of all, giving the nations the foundation of civilization. They can also be the most humble, taking up no space whatsoever among their hosts.

Heaven and Hell

Not only do we seek God's kingdom where it can readily be found, but even in the most unlikely place, like the exile, He can be found. And therefore at Mount Sinai God opened for them Heaven and Hell. No matter, He can be found there too.

From Zero to Aleph

Zero is nothing, and the opposite, a substantial number, is ten times ten, or one hundred. If you negate yourself before God, the one and only, represented by the letter *aleph*, it can be the doorway for all good deeds and blessings.

Never Learned

The more one feels lacking; yearns for new Torah and understanding; and stands at the door of the house of study as if just entering, as though he had never learned a word, the more he will receive great gifts from heaven.

Lower or Higher

On the one hand, a human being is nothing more than a creepy bit of protoplasm formed from bodily excretions; on the other hand, he is higher than the angels in heaven when he chooses to serve God. And only through the power of observing God's commandments can his inner nature be revealed.

Always Choosing

One who has climbed to a spiritual level higher than his neighbor should not be boastful. He too, no matter what height he has attained, stands before two paths, good and evil. He is no different from anyone else who also stands before the paths of good and evil.

God or the Worm

The purpose of the universe is the "crown" of the creation: man. Man was surely the first to be thought of, before any other creature, and last created, preceded even by the worm. And so we find nations that are dependent on the wormy, deep-in-the-ground levels of sorcery and magic, while the Jewish nation reverts to the roots in the primordial past of God's imagination.

Source of Energy

By negating all of one's energy before God, the source of all energy, wholesomeness, and peace, one reaches completion.

Personal Exodus

Each person, no matter how high he has climbed, no matter what he has accomplished, must remember his humble past, all the way back to the time he was nothing but some slimy protoplasm, cells dividing and forming. That memory is his personal exodus.

Surrendering

Handing over the very first of our toil and energies to God, completely and without reservation, even if only once a year, gives us more humility than an entire year of thrice-a-day prostrating ourselves before God.

Surrendering the first brings joy, and in its place only hardship can propel us to the same level.

One Point

One point of holiness, no matter how big or small, embraces the whole universe. Similarly, one Jew has to feel responsibility for every other Jew. And a *tzadik*, feeling this to the utmost, can save the entire nation. Only if one subordinates his being to the collective of the nation, and includes himself, is he, too, saved.

4

Above Nature

Yearning for God

Every individual has a speck of true yearning for God. And all our efforts in this earthly life are only to reveal that hidden truth. Thus man has within him all the holiness he will ever attain—concealed, yet within his reach.

From up Above

Abraham our forefather was lifted higher than the astrological spheres, rising above the physical. His offspring, too, descend from the celestial sphere and come to earth. As beings not of this world, they are able to assess the state of mankind and show them the way.

All Is One

The languages of the seventy nations are derived from Hebrew, the Holy Tongue. Seventy equals one. When the seventy recognize the one, they can also be one. Similarly, the forty-nine levels of wisdom are all contained in the singular fiftieth level. Forty-nine equals one. When we recognize the origin of all knowledge, our knowledge is unified. Number one is unique, deriving its power from the One and Only, God. Thus the word *ahavah*, love, has the same numerical value as *echad*, one. With love all is one.

Above Nature

Just as God leads His people above the rules of nature, they, too, follow him beyond their natural abilities. They break through all impediments and pursue God through thick and thin.

Feeble Man

Man is too feeble to receive the infinite light of God. Therefore he is bidden to observe God's commandments, through which he can have some connection to the spiritual world.

Up or Across

There are two paths leading to God: going high up to heaven, or crossing the wide ocean. Moses went up to heaven and brought down that first path with the Torah. Worshiping God with both desires—both good and evil—is the path of crossing the ocean.

A Narrow Funnel

God's gifts, in their spiritual form, are infinite. Man, who receives them, is as finite as a narrow funnel. And if he is worthy, God blesses him and enables him to receive whatever comes his way.

Changing

Nature is always changing and so are the fortunes of those who rely on their lucky stars and brute strength. Not so those who rise above that, yet lower themselves as the dust of the earth. They tap into the constant, permanent, and infinite providence of God.

Ex Nihilo

God created the world *ex nihilo*, making something from nothing. The work of the righteous is to return the something to nothing, the universe to God. And although it is a humanly impossible task, our great yearning brings success with God's help.

Breath of Prophecy

Just as God sees the past, present, and future, man too, with the breath that God breathed into him, can speak of the past, present, and future. That is prophecy, and the lower forms try to connect to it. The inanimate connects to the vegetative, the vegetable to the animal, the animal to man, then man to the Israelites, and the Israelites to the prophets.

Ancestors

Because our ancestors risked everything and broke through every barrier to rise to the heavens of spiritual levels, therefore we also share a fraction of their accomplishment. And only if we use all our energy to rise to the highest levels will our descendants have anything.

Paving the Paths

The greater minds, men and women of greater spirit, open the gates to the heavenly realms. Yet the plainer people, with their yearning, desire, and generosity, pave the paths for the heavenly spirit, making a way to all places and circumstances.

Not Knowing

The Torah teaches a person to fear and love God and enables him to produce fruit: deeds and students of his deeds. Yet all that is of secondary importance. The main gift of the Torah is received by not knowing, by the knowledge that it is beyond human understanding.

Root of Time

There are two realms of time: the natural, measurable time and the spiritual root of time, coming through the Torah, the Tree of Life.

Forty-Nine Gates

Man can strive and rise spiritually, level by level, through the forty-nine gates of wisdom. The fiftieth gate is beyond human capacity and impossible to enter. Still, once there, he receives a glimpse of it as a gift.

Leap across the Chasm

In order to receive the spirit of God, one must purify his heart. That purity comes from the Torah, which like a brook purifies everything immersed in it. Still, how does one get close to the Torah with an impure heart? By yearning for the Torah, we leap across the chasm and reach it.

Outer Light

The physical creation can receive a limited amount of light. That is the inner light. There is a great light, however, that cannot be contained but remains on the outside of the vessel. It is the surrounding light. One receives the inner light even for a limited performance. But the outer light is a gift for acts beyond one's capabilities.

Nearly an Angel

One can rise on the spiritual ladder and reach a level just below an angel's. But man will never be an angel, or perhaps only in death.

On His Level

Even Moses, the greatest Jewish prophet, did not possess the wisdom to understand God's teachings. Therefore God reviewed the Torah on his level.

Food Chain

There is a natural order: the inanimate, the vegetative, the animal, and man the communicator. He who lives on a materialistic level needs to be in the food chain. Those who are above it are sustained by the spiritual roots of nature, just as the Israelites were sustained by mana, a heavenly food.

Lamp of God

The World to Come is the spiritual part of this world. Each *mitzvah* that we do makes our body a lamp for the light of God revealed in that future world.

Means of Spirit

Just as the physical earth has mountains and valleys, clouds and rain, wind and dust, so too the spiritual world has our forefathers and the tribes, and other greats through whom our spiritual sustenance comes.

Not by Bread Alone

After receiving the mana in the desert, the Jewish people learned once and for all time that they do not live by bread alone. And unlike that of others, their attitude about food, money, and livelihood can rise above the base level of bodily needs.

Food of Rebellion

The full stomach of the servant causes him to rebel; therefore we thank God immediately as we partake in food. Thus we connect to the spiritual spark in the food and not to the outside husk, the illusion of the material world.

Space and Time

The first time God wrote the Ten Commandments on tablets of stone they did not need an Ark of the Covenant. They took up neither space nor time. The second time, after the sin of idolatry, an ark was needed.

Transgression

Man's transgression creates room for the curse. Otherwise he is free to choose and turn curse into blessing. How? While normally, step by step, the material world is far from God, we skip, and suddenly we stand before God.

Eyes to See

"The wise man has eyes in his head, while the fool walks in the darkness." The eyes are within the head so that man may look inward to find the root of his life and soul. But if he sees only up to his body and not beyond, then he is blind and looks only at the dead part of himself.

His goal is to reach the lofty world of the soul. Therefore he is not frightened of death, is undeterred by difficulties and pain, and pursues his goal: to reach the root of his soul.

Beyond Understanding

Man ought to judge every move, whether big or small, with understanding on the scales of truth. Then God grants him the ability to go beyond understanding directly to the truth.

Maturity

The Jewish people have all the requirements for spiritual maturity and do not need to look for it elsewhere, unlike others. They are likened to God, Whom they accept as their king and lord, and share in His completeness.

Measured Judgment

When the leaders of the generation are highly developed, they awaken in the hearts of each one the desire to use measured judgment and care.

Deceit

The world is full of deceit, lies, and quarrels. Honest judgment must therefore be out of this world. The world is finite, while truth is eternal and infinite and was placed in the care of Jacob and his descendants. And they have the power to call to another nation with peace and bring them nearer to the Creator.

Despite Wisdom

The Jewish nation was placed where the forces of nature are supreme and magic and sorcery dominate in order to raise them. Despite the attraction of worldly wisdom, they put it all aside to declare the name of God as king.

Matching

There is a spiritual order in the higher realms corresponding to the one below. Our task is to match our deeds to the order above. Actions that do not correspond to those above are sorcery and weaken our connection to that realm. In contrast, the Jewish people were taught to match their deeds perfectly with those of the spirit. Therefore they were given commandments in all facets of life, corresponding to the holiness in the heavenly realm: circumcision in the realm of the body, the Land of Israel and the Holy Temple in the realm of space, and the Sabbath in the realm of time.

Endless Understanding

Inside every item of creation there is the word of God. But it is not just the word, for layers upon endless layers of understanding that word are in there. Similarly, on our side, we can hear and understand more and more without limit.

"Natural" Miracles

At first God's miracles were unnatural; then they became part of the divine plan for the Jewish people.

Answer Amen

One who answers Amen in this world will merit to answer it in the next. If a person agrees to rise in spirit even without understanding, even if all that he can do is answer Amen, he will continue to go higher and higher.

Keep Going

When the door of your heart opens, do not stop and stare. It is only a hint of the possibilities at hand. Look for the next door and the next; enter and continue to enter.

On Earth

Man is like a ladder with its feet on the earth and its head in the heavens. So it is with the body and the soul: whatever man does on earth is reflected in his soul in heaven, and she basks in the spiritual delights.

Naturally above Nature

Although connected to the highest spheres above the physical world, the Jewish people are physical and live within nature. Yet they have the opportunity to raise not only nature but even the astrological influences. They raise them to a higher plane and free them from immutable laws.

5

Chosen People

Eternal People

The eternal nature of the Jewish people is irrefutable. No matter how horrible a campaign of annihilation our enemies plan, in the end the Jewish people prevail and begin to regenerate. We have been witness to this truth in the fifty years since the Holocaust. We must never be embarrassed of our hope for redemption, because it always comes.

Stars

The Jewish people are compared to a star in Hebrew, *kochav*, comprised of the letters *chof beis* and *chof vav*. *Chof beis* represents the twenty-two letters of the Hebrew alphabet used in the Creation, while *chof vav* equals twenty-six as the numerical value of God's name. Thus we are composed of both earthly and celestial energies.

Channel for Peace

Only one vessel among all the vessels is flawless because it is divine: peace. The Jewish people who were blessed with peace are therefore the channel for all blessings. Whoever wants peace should bless them with peace.

Flowers of the Nations

Just as the royal gardener upon seeing a beautiful flower acquires it for his master, so too the righteous among the nations are hand-picked to join the nation of God.

Suffering Nations

The Jewish people, through their communication—writings and speaking—cause the nations of the world to recognize God. And when the nations oppress them, not only do the Jewish people suffer, but the oppressors suffer spiritually, too, by not receiving guidance from their victims.

Training

Although man instinctively runs from danger, God did not allow the Jewish people to run. He deliberately took them through the most dangerous places to train and teach them. Although their paths will be filled with danger, they will persevere and prevail.

Resolved

The essence of the Jewish people's mission at Mount Sinai was to establish the truth of God's kingdom and sovereignty throughout the world in every place and in all circumstances.

Always

Just as God was in the past, will be in the future, and is in the present, so are the Jewish people.

God Is Truth

God is truth and rests His presence on a man of truth. And He named Jacob *Yisro-el*, adding God's name, signifying that God rests His name on them.

Unaffected

No curse can befall the entire Jewish people unless they stumble into sin. And even then, sin does not become part of their essence. The holiness of their soul leaves them before they sin and is thus unaffected by evil.

Awakening

Because the Jewish people are chosen to serve God, their very first act upon arising is to declare God's kingdom.

Unique

Compared to the other nations the Jewish people are very few in number. Their uniqueness is not at first apparent. They are the source of blessing, the hiddenmost spiritual place, protected from the jealous stares of the wicked.

Poetic Censure

The prophet's task is to raise the Jewish people, through his prayer and poetic censure, from the potential to the actual. Just as man's speech is an expression of his character, so too is that of the prophet. His prophecy is an expression of the character of the Jewish people in that moment of history.

Jacob and Israel

The Jewish people live on two planes. One level is Jacob, who lived with his wicked brother and father-in-law and still established his integrity and honesty. Similarly, the Jewish people live as a Torah nation among the nations. Then there is the level of Israel, who have their own land and a way of life shared by no one else in the world.

Offshoots

As soon as the nations attain a bit of spirituality, they think that they will surpass the Jewish people. But that is hardly possible, since they are but offshoots of Jewish teachings.

Elevating the Everyday

Although the Jewish people are involved in everyday affairs, this is in order to elevate them. And their joy derives from being left alone to complete their task.

Channels of Prosperity

The nations complain that the Jewish people prevent heavenly blessings from reaching them. In everyday language, they say that the Jews are too rich, too talented, and too smart, and that they take everything for themselves. But the truth is that they are the channel for all blessings. And in every country where the Jews prosper, the entire country prospers with them. It has been that way throughout history.

Abraham's Light

At first, God's light descended to all the nations. After Abraham rose to declare God's kingdom, he became the channel for that light.

Truth and Peace

Truth and peace, in a world of falsehood, can be found only with great effort and God's help. And the Jewish people acquire those two virtues with the help of the Torah of truth and by pursuing peace to the utmost. It is so much a part of them that they are always able to reach out to all the nations and greet them with truth and peace.

Closer and Closer

All the nations are able, through their good deeds, to get close to God. The Jewish people, however, were chosen for higher responsibility. They do God's will in order to be closer to Him, to serve Him always more deeply, and to get even closer to Him.

Congregation

Each tribe is a congregation, and all of them together comprise the congregation of Jacob. Jacob unites all of them.

Face to Face

God and the Jewish people are face to face; God "turns away" from all other concerns, and so do His people, and they are absorbed only with each other.

Filters

The Jewish people are the vessels through whom the Torah filters into the world. Their spiritual energy attracts the nations and they come to join them.

No Matter What

The special relationship of God and the Jewish people, called *Anochi*, never leaves them. And therefore they always recognize Him. And no matter who may contradict them, they adhere to Him, as a birth-mother, no matter what, holds onto her child.

Dispersed Sparks

Divine, holy sparks are dispersed throughout the world. The mission of the Jewish people is to find and uplift them to a higher realm. They can do this with the power of the Torah. Or, if not worthy, they must go into exile to gather them.

Double Renewal

Just as every individual gets renewed each day, the *klal*, the community, gets renewed also. By subordinating himself to the community, the individual gains double renewal.

Torah's Life

The Jewish people gave up all other life and desired life only from the Torah. In response, the Torah gave life to all their limbs and sinews and made them new.

Messengers

The Jewish people are the messengers who relate God's message and teachings to all mankind.

Without Deeds

The way we conceive God is the way He responds to us. And since the Jewish people came to Him without deeds but ready to follow, God, too, responds to them in kind; they are chosen regardless of their deeds.

On Their Own

Although man can reach the highest levels through miracles, the Jewish people want to rise spiritually on their own.

Handles of Vessels

Each nation and language is spiritually opposite the Jewish people and their language. Yet by teaching the Torah in all the languages they function as the handles for the vessels of the Torah, and it fills them all with wisdom.

Lifting the Hearts

The deeds of any Jew affect the spiritual state of the righteous. Therefore, when the *tzadik* feels a need for repentance and repents, he is able to lift up the hearts of the common folk and make them yearn for repentance too.

More Serious

The Jewish people are in a very dangerous position. Since they are so close to God, their sins are more serious than those of any human on earth, and their punishment and suffering are also beyond the pale of humanity. Yet their stature and importance are beyond measure or human understanding. Therefore they need great protection.

Never Consumed

The Torah is like fire and must take hold on a substance. If the substance is straw, like the nations, it is consumed, and in an instant the fire is gone. The Jewish people, however, who cleave to God the infinite, are never consumed by the fire.

High and Low

When the Jewish people are high, they are very high, but when they are low, no one is lower. And do not think that the peak of their character is seen at the top, in their own land. On the contrary, their beauty shines in their humble state in the exile.

The Code

No mortal could possibly fulfill the lofty code of conduct of God's will. Still, God has chosen the Jewish people for that difficult task. Their essence fits the code and the code fits their essence. They inevitably fall short of their duty, and God brings them near with repentance.

Force of One

The nations receive their needs through the forces of celestial spheres, the zodiac, while the Jewish people receive from the One and Only. It is their faith that teaches others that nature is not the force of many but the force of one.

Eternal Love

Because the Jewish people are ready to sacrifice, to give up all their possessions, their desires, their very life for God, their love of Him is independent of any thing and is therefore eternal.

Character Witnesses

Who can be a character witness? Only one without attachments. Thus the Jewish people, who give their very life away for God's will, neither ask for nor await any reward and are therefore true witnesses for the kingdom of God.

For Others

The nations, even when they do for others, do for themselves. The Jewish people, on the other hand, even when asking for themselves, really only want God's kingdom to be revealed.

The Hidden One

First is the first in a series of numbers, but *one* has no beginning and no end, and is the one and only God. We do not readily see Him, because nature hides Him within the limits of space and time. The Jewish people, however, by accepting His kingdom, experience Him even within nature.

Knowledge and Deeds

The overflowing knowledge of the wise men and women of the nations inadvertently causes them to do some good deeds. The Jewish people, on the other hand, because of their abundant good deeds, gain wisdom and understanding.

Choosing to Proclaim

A king has the power to frighten everyone. God allowed mankind to choose His fear freely. But who will choose it? The Jewish people choose and proclaim Him as the king. And when they do, all join in the choosing and proclamation.

Despite It All

Praised is he who realizes that he is part of the chosen people, elevated with great responsibilities. And even more praised is he who, despite it all, humbles himself to the very earth before the Creator.

Down to Earth

The Jewish people are witnesses that God created the universe and He is its master. Because of their lofty spiritual state, however, they would normally be unable to convey this message to the rest of mankind. It is only by descending to Egypt, and being dragged through the basest of labor and suffering and then being redeemed, that they are able to relate to nations who worship the material world.

Children

The Jewish people are called the children of God when they separate from the nations and unite as one.

The King's Sons

The blessing comes if you listen to God's commandments, and the curse, if you do not listen. They are two paths, a crossroads, for the servants of the king. The sons of the king, however, follow him and are never in doubt.

Testimony

The Jewish people are witnesses, and they establish God's kingdom with their testimony. The more they delve, and investigate, and dig up the facts to get to the truth, the more believable and valuable is their testimony. The entire process is judgment, evoking a response of loving kindness from God.

Their Deeds

Although other nations are influenced by their stars and angels in heaven, the Jewish people have risen above that. When the Israelites at Mount Sinai answered God with the words "we will do and we will listen," they affirmed that their fate will depend on their deeds. Therefore they are never satisfied in spotting a gift from God. They would rather earn and deserve it.

Ten or Ten

The world was created with ten commands, and all power from the material world is from that source. The Jewish people, on the other hand, accepted more responsibility and get their energy from the Ten Commandments.

It is far easier to listen to the ten commands, the outer and apparent part of everything. But they put that aside in favor of the spiritual reality within.

Are the Nations Willing?

If the nations were willing, the Jewish people could bring them before the throne of God and cause peace to be accepted throughout the world.

Is Knowledge Power?

If knowledge is power, then all mankind shares in three kinds of power: power of time, as with astrologers, astronomers, and meteorologists who advise which time is most suitable; power of activity, as with politicians, industrialists, and economists who advise which activities are suitable; and power of the psyche, as with psychologists, public-relations counselors, and propagandists who advise on the workings of the human mind. The Jewish people, however, have the letters of the Torah planted in their hearts, and are able to connect their life to those letters. They are able to change, to raise the spiritual level of all the powers, and to use them in the service of God.

Might

The other nations rule with the power of their bodies, while the Jewish people derive their power by subordinating their body to the soul. And when they do that, their soul can overpower the might of the nations.

Join the Group

The Jewish people as a group always stand before God. Then why are we not there? We need merely to subordinate our being to the rest of the nation, and then we will be there, too. By this means all the wicked can return to God. The evil in them is but temporary, an accident, and not part of them. All they need to do is drop their wicked crust, and inside they are as shiny as the newest silver.

Without Deeds

The way we conceive God is the way He responds to us. And since the Jewish people came to Him without deeds but ready to follow, God, too, responds to them in kind; they are chosen regardless of their deeds.

The Chosen People

The greatest knowledge and most important thing to know is
that God has chosen the Jewish people. That fact is greater,
higher, and beyond what any one person has ever accomplished. Rather than think of his deeds, one should subordinate himself to his people as a whole, the chosen ones. So
we wonder: how could anyone think that he is better than any
other person? Isn't one member just as important in God's
eyes as any other?

Each and Every

Why are the Jewish people counted in the Torah? Are they
not without number? The Torah teaches that each and every
one of them has a number and is special, and that no two can
accomplish the same task.

Chosen

God has chosen the entire creation, and He has chosen the
Jewish people. And when the love for them is revealed, no
sin nor accusation can disturb it.

Our Ancestors

God chose our ancestors, and we are the inheritors of their spirit. Thus surely the spirit of the Jewish people is near God. Then why do we not feel close to Him? It must be the physical self that separates us, but with fear and awe of Him the inner Jewishness is revealed.

Three Levels

There are three levels in the relationship of God and the Jewish people. The highest level is that the Jewish people are the children of God, close to Him and able to speak with Him directly; they are also a holy nation and God is their king; and the third level is that God chose each one and the entire nation of Israel. Still, this is a very high spiritual level.

Poverty and Riches

The spiritual challenge of poverty is to remain steadfast in our faith and trust in God. On the other hand, the challenge of riches is not to discard our faith in the face of accomplishment. The spiritual challenge of riches is even greater than that of poverty. And those who stand up to the latter challenge will have the strength to overcome the harder one.

6

Revealing the Hidden

Witness

Just as a court witness is questioned about his knowledge of the minutest details, those who want to be witnesses to the Creator need to know clearly who and where they are, and what their goal is.

To the Heavens

Heaven is really on the earth, too. It is only the evil of the wicked that blinds us to the realization of God's presence. Thus, the people whose deeds bring God's presence to earth are elevated to the heavens.

Dual Nature

The Jewish people have both a concealed and a revealed nature. Their root, named *Yaakov*, the hidden heel of their souls, is connected to their forefathers and foremothers. Their day-to-day life, named *Yisroel*, being straight with God, is the act of revealing God's kingdom.

Is He Hidden?

If the kingdom of God is revealed, then there is no choice or free will. Thus, to allow for free will, the kingdom of God is concealed. Once the choice is made, man discovers just where He was hidden. Or did it only seem that way?

Spiritual

Although concealed, God's spirituality is present in each item of creation. Just as there is a physical body, in that same space hovers a spiritual body. And those who tune in to it find God in the world.

Precious Stones

Diamonds, precious stones, and pearls all come from hidden places. The Torah is more precious than any of them. Not only is she holy from her place of origin, but she cleanses and enlightens everything around her. Not only is she the princess in the palace's inner chamber, but she goes forth to the streets and brings the ways of royalty to everyone she meets.

Truth Awakened

When man does a deed entirely for God's sake, for the revelation of His kingdom, that is the truth, and therefore truth is awakened and revitalized.

Prison

Man's body without spirit is in a spiritual prison. Observing *mitzvos* creates a channel for Torah's light to enter the body and free it from prison. Similarly, on a larger scale, when the Jewish people become lamps and radiate with Torah's light, they liberate Jerusalem from her prison.

Light

The way one sits, walks, and talks in the darkness is the sort of light revealed to him.

Lest You Drown

A person can forget the spiritual light within him. By doing a *mitzvah* he remembers, and that memory lingers. Without it, he is in mortal danger, just like a drowning man. He must quickly hold on to a *mitzvah*.

---

613 Energies

Just as the Torah has 613 commandments outside man's body, there are also 613 sorts of spiritual energy inside his body. In the observation of a *mitzvah*, a particular energy is awakened.

Projection

If one feels inferior, he projects that image onto others and they also perceive him that way. Man can work to reveal his infinite spiritual nature, thereby determining how he perceives himself.

Hidden Protector

Man needs protection. He can protect himself by either physical or spiritual means. Physical protection has a dark side: it hides God's omniscience. Similarly, God's protection, being spiritual, is also hidden. When worthy, the Jewish people experience God's protection and the forces of darkness recede to the background.

Home

The greatest joy is when a creature returns to its roots. There it is home, nurtured by its original energy, in serenity and peace.

Attached

Angels remain at their original spiritual level, while man moves higher and higher. Even man, however, is not able to ascend, if he is attached to and imprisoned by the material world.

A New Place

The world is full of God's honor, and hence a sinner, by attempting to evict God, has no place in the world. And if he recognizes and agonizes over the fact that he has no place, God gives him a new place.

Particular Light

The primordial light hidden at creation is the reward for the righteous in the World to Come. It is hidden in infinite ways in a man's lifetime. For each individual, another aspect of the light is waiting, and similarly hidden. Thus there is a particular hiddenness and struggle in your life, so that you may reach the light in the next world.

In Man's Lust

The World to Come is hidden in the present world, in man's lust for the physical. It is spiritual and cannot be found or discerned. The task is to uncover the hidden in every item and then to relate to the eternal and infinite within, instead of using the divine for the sake of the material world.

Dig We Must

Although fountains and brooks dot the hills, one can find water after digging to the water table. Thus water is everywhere to be found. In some places it is accessible, while elsewhere one must work hard to attain it. The Torah, too, is everywhere, but the Jewish people work hard to uncover it.

Eyes to See

God puts the sustenance of every creature before them, to some in a hidden manner, and to others revealed. When God opens one's eyes, one sees everything he needs. Thus, when there is unity, and the energy is flawless, one is able to see what he needs.

Deep Taste

The taste of the natural world is on the surface, while the taste of the spiritual world is hidden and waiting to be uncovered.

Light and Darkness

The night is a mixture of light and darkness. Morning separates the light from the darkness, and by the afternoon it is clearly and only light.

Doing and Speaking

Although the world was created with ten commands, it is called the act of creation. It is connected more to doing than to speaking. The Torah, however, is the Ten Commandments, the spoken word of God to His people.

Finding His Name

The name of God gives strength. One can find His name in the Torah, composed entirely of names of God in different combinations.

Lives They Live

There is a part of the Torah concealed within its words. It is the echo of God's words as He speaks to mankind. Those who respond and speak up with the lives they live, reveal its secrets.

Secret and Revealed

There is in the Torah that which must be heard before it is understood. There is also that which cannot be heard. It is understood because of the Torah etched in our hearts. The former and the latter are the revealed and the secret teachings, and they unite to form one Torah.

Torah Principles

The Torah and its commandments are the means to reveal that nature is organized according to Torah principles.

Chosen to Follow

Nature follows natural laws. The Jewish people, however, have been raised above the natural and respond to divine laws. But how do their natural brains have the sense to follow God? Because God chose them and leads them, they follow Him as an animal follows its master.

Expanding the Mind

How is it possible for a creature to be a witness that God is Lord, King of the universe? It is only because his witnessing is truth, and the truth causes an expansion of his mind with greater understanding and intelligence.

The End

The source of each thing is in the heavenly realm, the loftiest of spiritual levels. The further it is from the source, the weaker it is spiritually. And that is what God wants from us: to connect the end to its beginning.

Introduction

The introduction to all events is the awe of God. If we possess it, we know that He is the cause of all events. But without it, a layer of concealment covers the truth.

Wherever You Turn

The world was created for God's honor, and therefore one can find a *mitzvah*, a good deed, in every item of the creation. And one who yearns and seeks *mitzvos* will find them in every place and every time.

Sublime Reward

We are familiar with this material world. Yet right below the surface is a world of atomic particles, forces, and energy fields. That world is of an entirely different sort. So is the World to Come, the sublime world of the final reward and punishment.

God's sublime reward for His loyal servants cannot be received in this state of reality. It awaits them in the future state, in *Olam Haba*, the World to Come. On the other hand, the wicked are rewarded for their good deeds in this world. They receive their deserved reward, but in a finite and passing state, while the righteous will enjoy everlasting bliss.

Observing the commandments creates a spiritual light that, in the future, will transform the organs of the body. With that sublime body we will be able to enjoy God's reward in the World to Come.

God Is Present

Not only did God not leave the earth, but He recreates the universe each day and renews the primordial Ten Commandments. And the channel for it all is the Torah, whose light is the life of the universe.

Dreams

In order for man to receive spiritual energy it is clothed in a physical garment. Just as the kernel of wheat carrying energy to those who eat it is clothed in the husk, messages from heaven are clothed in dreams. And that admixture must be sifted and separated to get the most use from its energy.

Inner Wisdom

The wisdom of God permeates the universe inside and outside. The manifest laws of nature, describing how things happen, provide man with great wisdom. That wisdom is real and
wonderful and is available to all of mankind. Still, how much
greater is the wisdom of the inner workings, the spiritual portion of all things! That portion can be learned from the Torah
and reaches beyond the wisdom gathered from nature.

In Freedom

We must attempt to liberate the holy sparks, the spirit within
the material exile, while we are free men. Once the enemy,
the evil urge, engages us in battle, all our energy will be taken
up with attempting to overpower it.

Light from Afar

The world was created with a great light that lit up the universe from one end to the other. God hid that light and sends
some of its rays to light the path of the righteous. Similarly,
the soul of man is kept in a heavenly abode, while its light
shines into the life of those who observe the commandments.

Action and Reaction

Each of The Torah's commandments is active in the spiritual realm, but it takes man's action to complete it. With man's action on earth and God's "action" in heaven, the deed is accomplished. The light from heaven gets attached to a particular organ of the body. And once uplifted and filled with light, that organ is ready to do another *mitzvah*.

All One

Although the commandments are manifest in different ways and deal with different parts of the body, in Adam, the first human being, they were all united as one command. Because he sinned, they became separated into many.

The goal then is to unify all of them. Can they then be weighed and measured to see which gets a greater reward? No, they are all one and the same, united to establish God's kingdom.

Removing the Sheath

All the commandments are similar to circumcision: to remove the sheath, the material covering, from every part of the body and to reveal the inner spirit, God's commandments. Each of them is a key fitting another organ to attach it to the spiritual realm. But the key is also for opening the treasure-houses in those organs, with their great spiritual treasures.

Light in the Darkness

Is it merely an illusion to think of renewal? The truth is that God's light, His holy spark within every item of creation, is never aging and always new. Yet that newness is hidden below the surface and revealed through our good deeds. But aren't deeds themselves of the material world of darkness? How, then, is the new revealed? It is the power of the Torah's commandments to bring renewal even within our physical deeds and through them to reveal the new in all things.

Doors within Doors

The door that opens in our heart is a reflection of the heavenly door. Just as the body reflects the soul, the *tfilin* worn on our head during prayer are a reflection of the *tfilin* inside our head, energized by our physical *tfilin*. As a reward, not only does the spirit of man shine forth, but also his physical body—a door within a door.

No End

Whatever has a beginning also has an end and is therefore finite and incomplete. Therefore the Jewish people give away the beginning of all their assets to God. Thus without a beginning the enterprise has no end either. It becomes infinite.

Like the Blind

The Jewish people were created to bring light to the world by observing the commandments. Otherwise the opacity of the body hides the light. And especially in the darkness of the exile, how can we hope to be guided by the light of the Torah? We are like the blind who use their sense of touch to find their way. We, too, feel and sense where the light of the Torah may be, although we do not see it directly. Then God helps us find our way.

Partners

When we do a good deed, only the outside, the physical aspect, is ours, the inner part of the deed is God's. We ought to think about that before observing the commandments. We are about to strike a partnership with God. We and God are doing something together. With a partner like that, how ought we to act?

The More You See

The more you strive to reveal the kingdom of God in each thing and circumstance, the more you see that it is so. On the other hand the wicked, who conceal God's kingdom, walk in darkness.

Limits

A creation, by definition, must have measure and boundaries. That is what distinguishes it as a creature and is sustained by the Creator. The Jewish people declare God's kingdom and place all creatures within their measured places. Thus they have life.

Worthless Metals

All precious metals become worthless when the inner light of the Torah is revealed. But the real and true remains with its original value.

Creative Commands

The creative commands of God hover above the material world and energize those who perform the *mitzvos*.

Focus on Divine Light

We experience doubt from the external part of a situation. If we focus on God's light, concealed below the surface, clarity results, and we know what to do.

The Twenty-Two Letters

The universe was created with the twenty-two letters of the Hebrew alphabet. And for each human being there are letters that speak directly and exclusively to him. They are the address of his life's mission and challenges. And each day the letters radiate with a new combination of auras, giving man new life and insight. And when one tunes in to the newness of each of his life's days, the entire creation becomes renewed with him.

7

Path of the Righteous

Out of Bounds

To the degree that the *tzadik* is ready to be a channel for spiritual energy, that is the measure of holiness, unfettered by space and time, that he receives.

Lust of the Righteous

Both the wicked and the righteous have lust. The wicked lust for their wickedness, and the righteous for the highest spiritual levels. By yearning to reach the roots of their souls, the righteous rise higher and higher to the ultimate.

Even the Righteous

The wicked remove themselves from the World to Come because of their lust. In contrast, the lust of the righteous removes them from the confusion of the material world as they rush to cleave to the world of spirit. They are the foundation of the earth, while the wicked are a mere sprouting of grass on that foundation.

Protecting the Light

Spiritual light is extinguished by the evil deeds of the wicked. Still, the righteous deeds of the tzadikim resist the darkness. They are like a shield in face of the raging waters, and they prevail.

Truth Is Pure

Truth is its own witness. And thus the true servant of God fills with joy when he is able to serve God with a wholly pure heart.

Friend to Sinners

The righteous follow the path of Aaron the High Priest and befriend even the sinners, who, in their embarrassment, return to God's ways.

Inclusion

Even if one is genuinely elevated above the ordinary folks by great deeds, still he needs to include himself with the others. He has to know that his extraordinariness is not in being excluded, but being included and raising the masses to new heights.

The Tzadik

Even the evil urge yearns to be in the control of the *tzadik*.

Both Are Needed

One who approaches God's commandments with simplicity and without strategies is often able to accomplish more than even the *tzadik*. On the other hand, the intentions of the righteous are much more spiritual, even if the results are more meager. God combines the two and completes the *mitzvah* for each one.

Trifling Deeds

Even a lifelong *tzadik*, standing before the heavenly tribunal, will be ashamed of his trifling deeds. And because of his shame they will be accepted.

Perseverance

One who is righteous in all ways will surely receive his reward in the World to Come. One who has gone astray, however, and is now devoted to God, must persevere. He must not allow himself to be defeated by evil. He must answer his lusts and desires by saying, "Let the morning come and we'll see whom the King really likes!" Because if one is His servant, God causes circumstances to happen to insure his success.

―――――――――

Channel

The *tzadik*, because of his righteousness, has great merit. He channels blessings to the world so as to enhance life and avoid death, especially murder. With his fervent prayer he influences even the evil forces not to harm others.

―――――――――

Trust or Sorcery

All day long things are happening. God's servant has full trust in His providence as the events unfold. One with less trust turns to sorcery to influence the outcome. With magic he wishes to change that which has been decreed. But the servant's trust will serve him well, and he will be shown the divine plan, which even angels are wont to see.

Prophets

Just as the people need their prophets, the prophets need the people. And to show their righteousness, God removes prophets from among the people.

Opportunities

The righteous are busy every moment of the day, showering mankind with kindness, whereas the wicked are looking every second for opportunities for their wickedness.

New Light

The righteous subordinate their will to God's will and hope for His kindness. Therefore a new light is revealed to them each day.

Increasing

The wicked spread the darkness of the material world. On the other hand, the business of the righteous is to increase spiritual light. Both work with equal fervor, diligence, and enthusiasm.

Tones of Love

The meaning of a sentence changes with the tone in which it is said. Similarly, when the righteous are aware of the future, they endow it with love and compassion. And through them the event changes for the better.

Painful Truth

The more the righteous uncover the divine light dwelling in all things, the more the eyes of the wicked are in pain from looking at the truth.

Grabbing

Materialistic people grab whatever they see to please their appetite. They do not even survey what is before them. On the other hand, those who want to rise above nature find the source of the divine in everything.

With Actions

There is the witness who has to state his testimony, and there is one who does not have to say anything. Instead, he is a witness by his being and his actions.

Real Leaders

Although some spiritual leaders are on the highest level, they can nevertheless draw the entire people with them, while others need to cater to their followers.

———————

Follow the Tzadik

Although one cannot reach the high spiritual level of the *tzadik*, one should still cleave to him, as we were taught, "Be the tail to a lion, and not the head of a fox."

———————

The Altar

The heavens were split into upper and lower waters. The lower ones cry because of their distance from God but are reassured that they will be brought near, poured on the altar. Similarly, there are souls who cry about their distance from God. For them, God provides the *tzadik* who brings them close. He is the altar for those souls.

———————

Important Deeds

The righteous are too humble to consider their deeds important enough to be mentioned. The conceited are otherwise.

Abundant Life

Just as one who supports scholars of the Torah is rewarded with life in abundance, so too if one speaks words of Torah, his tongue is healed.

Gates

All the great Torah scholars have the power to open the gates of understanding to the Torah and its commandments.

The Seventy-Two Righteous

We must be connected to God to have real life. If we sin, the connection weakens. There are grave sins that are enough to sever the connection entirely. Similarly, the Jewish people are connected through the seventy-two righteous of the generation. And because of their sins, the seventy-two are split in half, thirty-six *tzadikim* for *Eretz Yisroel* and thirty-six in the diaspora. There are also thirty-six in heaven and thirty-six on earth. With repentance, however, all is set right again.

Undeserving

Just as God desires that the righteous should earn what they receive with their good deeds, the righteous are happier receiving gifts from God for no reason. They would rather be humble and feel truly undeserving.

Afraid

In time of danger, the righteous believe and are confident in God's help. Yet they humble themselves till they are actually afraid of the danger. They know that they do not deserve miracles and therefore must do everything normally and naturally.

Do Not Fear

Even if at first you are afraid of the problem and the threat, trust in God and do not fear. No matter how many layers upon layers of concealment prevent you from seeing the hand of God, you must be strong and not be afraid. Even if you are by nature timid and cowardly, do not fear.

Even Moses

Moses our teacher was always in awe of God. After all, he spoke with Him face to face. Thus when he brought down the Torah from Mount Sinai and presented it to the Jewish people, he also gave himself. They inherited his lofty spirit and awe along with the Torah.

Challenges

Just as there are infinite opportunities to rise higher in spirit, so too there are infinite new and unexpected challenges to upset the servant of God.

Search for Truth

What is the root of righteousness and truth? It is God Him-self, the God of truth. And therefore in our quest for truth there is no point at which we stop and say, "We searched enough, and we have arrived at the ultimate truth." Just as it is not possible to fathom God, so it is with the truth. We must con-stantly and forever be searching for it.

Awakening Heart

God always desires the righteousness of every human being. There are times, however, that are more conducive to the awakening of man's heart. With a nudge from heavens above, he suddenly experiences compassion and pity for his poor soul descending from her lofty home and now sinking into the quicksand of the physical world.

Hearts

The prophet gets his heart from the collective heart of the Jewish people, and therefore his words, coming from his heart, go directly into theirs.

Dead or Alive

The righteous focus all their bodily energy into the immortal spirit inside them and are "alive" even in death. The wicked, on the other hand, subordinate their souls to the mortal body and are therefore considered "dead" even in life.

Establishing the Kingdom

The King asked his many gardeners to care for his orchard. Each was rewarded according to the difficulty or ease of his work, depending on which trees and greenery he cared for. But all of them, as a group, were rewarded for establishing the King's orchard, an accomplishment that is more than its parts.

Similarly, each person will be rewarded for observing the commandments, according to his deeds. The greatest reward, however, will be for establishing the kingdom of God by observing the commandments. And that reward will be equal for all, regardless of the difficulty or ease of the work.

As If

God has already made everything, and it is all complete. The righteous, however, bring creation out of its potential to the actual, as if they made it. That is far greater in God's eyes than anything else.

Without Attention

Everyone does good deeds without even paying attention to them. The righteous are rewarded for them, and the wicked lose them in the darkness of the material world. When the light of the Sabbath shines in, we realize our loss and search for it.

By Faith Alone

If one is a *tzadik*, righteous through and through, and still lives by his faith, as if he had never done a good deed, and thinks that if not for his faith he would have nothing, his deeds will last.

Beginning Portion

God created the universe so that He has a beginning portion of it, and they are the Jewish people. Although there are millions and billions of galaxies, nothing establishes His kingdom as His people do. They are the witnesses who actually proclaim His kingdom, and cause others to do the same, so that even if the entire human race is wicked or denies God, there still is the beginning portion, who tenaciously continue to witness for Him.

We were created in this lowly world; still, it is the house of God and therefore gets renewed each day, and we praise Him for it. Because You made us poor, You lift us up.

Oil and Water

Just as oil does not mix with other liquids, so too the *tzadik* with Torah absorbed in his veins does not mix with evil. And just as oil, even when mixed with other liquids, floats to the top, so too the repentant sinner, who was already mixed with evil, still can rise to the top.

Who Is Higher?

The righteous *tzadik* is higher than the repentant sinner in some aspects, and the repentant sinner is higher than the righteous person in others. The *tzadik* follows God's path always without exception, and occasionally even experiences a great revelation. His fear of God is tempered by participation in life, since he is of both the earth and heaven. The repentant sinner, on the other hand, could not repent on his own and needed God to help him. He is literally held up by God. Therefore who could compare to him? Still, he is not there on his own.

Material Pleasures

The *tzadik*, whose life is pure and holy, cannot have true joy from sheer material pursuits. On the other hand, the wicked person can enjoy the material world. The repentant sinner is different. Because he struggled to find God's path, he reached the realm of the World to Come and can enjoy the pleasures of the material world without adverse effects.

The righteous, although high in spirit, may revert to sin if they receive the physical joys of the world. The repentant, however, has already learned to walk on that path and is rendered harmless to them.

Our Heritage

We are descendants of our great forefathers and foremothers. But despite our heritage, could we ever hope to live a noble life as they did? The best we can do is to imitate in some small measure the type of life they lived. Then God in His mercy will do the rest.

God's Kindness

The righteous awaken, so to speak, God's kindness and love for His creatures. And while the wicked may rant and rave to fill the world with darkness, they cannot overpower God's love for the world.

Lower Level

Although the *tzadikim*, the flawlessly righteous, live on the level of truth, they must find a way to relate to others who live on the level of faith, a lower spiritual level.

Like a Bride

The righteous are like a bride, modest in her parents' home, but at the wedding everyone knows her. They too are modest as the dust of the earth, but everyone knows them for their good deeds.

8

Purity of Heart

Illusions

It is difficult to fashion a vessel from silver containing impurities. Similarly, man too must rid himself of his illusions before he receives God's blessings.

Direct Connection

All creatures have stood in awe of God and responded to His command since the days of creation, except man. He had lost this simple, direct connection on account of sin. Only by subordinating his will to God's will can man hope to break through all barriers and stand directly before God.

All True

God is the God of truth, and truth is forever and everywhere true in any and every circumstance. And to the extent that we understand this, that is how directly God reveals his truth to us.

Precede Evil

If you do not rise in the morning with the explicit desire to be a humble servant of God, you can be sure that a wicked person is up before you and with jealousy and arrogance is cursing anyone who has anything that he wants.

Pure Seed

Everyone has a word or a letter in the Torah, and it is the divine spark of his soul, never defiled. The seed from which man is formed imparts impurity, yet the baby born from it is pure because of the soul that enters its body. The Torah, too, purifies all who study it.

Purity

All defilement and uncleanliness is made pure by uniting with the One and Only. In Him all becomes clean. When wisdom leads to humility before God, it leads to purity, too—not the desire to be wisest of men, but the wisdom and understanding of God.

Stepping Down

The written Law is etched into stone with force, while the oral Law grows from the heart of the congregation of Israel. And when the force is too much for the masses, one must step down to bring them up to the higher level.

Lasting Value

One can have immediate gratification from the Torah, like one who has just eaten honey. Still, that is temporary. Soon the effect of that taste fades and it is gone. And one can also experience the Torah as gold, a metal of lasting value, with no end in sight.

Harmonious Organism

In nature, the male and the female are opposites, yet they unite to form a new, independent, harmonious organism. Similarly, each human being has his own opinion and approach, perhaps opposite to that of others, in understanding the Torah. If he can drop his bias and seek only the truth, God will open his eyes and the truth will be revealed.

Beginning to End

Anyone can serve God, but to serve Him with truth is possible only with the Torah's commandments. Only the Torah is a fusion of the past and the future, from the beginning to the end.

United in Love

The Torah is the root of all the Jewish souls, and in her their unity is found. And when they are united, each can love the other as he loves himself.

No Erasing

Just as there are names of God that we are forbidden to erase, similarly there are also names, God's divine sparks in us, that are impossible to erase.

Difficult Challenges

You would think that the higher one rises in spirituality, the easier it becomes. But it is not so. Each new level comes with more and more difficult challenges.

Torah's Fragrance

One must be in the realm of freedom to receive the Torah. And even if one is unprepared, he still picks up the fragrance, like one entering a spice store.

Resonating

The commandments are lamps, and the Torah is the bright-est light, dimming the light of the lamps. That light resonates in every part of man's body and prepares him for action.

Primordial Light

The inner nature of creation is the primordial light hidden by God for a future time. And it is the light of the Torah.

Mending Sin

Each generation inherits the spiritual merit and virtue attained by the previous one. But then they also have to mend the sins of that generation.

Ordinary Life

The Torah is full of stories so that its holiness can spread and take hold of the ordinary life of each person.

Healing Language

Languages have descended into the abyss of defilement be-cause they are used for wickedness. But the holy tongue, the language of the Torah, is healed because it is used for holiness.

Soft and Glowing

Iron, although stiff, hard, and dark, when heated becomes soft and glowing. Similarly, the *yetzer hora*, the inclination to evil, stubborn and materialistic, when heated with the fire of Torah becomes pliable and glows with the light of the spirit.

Never to Forget

The act of a *mitzvah* fills man with holiness and prepares him to receive the Torah. And therefore it is even more important not to indulge in prohibited behavior, so as not to forget the Mount Sinai experience.

Living Words

Not only is God alive, always and forever, His words and commandments are alive, too. Thus the commandments are actually alive inside of each heart. The more one purifies his heart, the more he feels the life of the commandments.

Who Is Near?

Those who boast that they are the closest to God, are not, while those who express concern about how far they are from Him, are near.

Partners

Nothing is perfect, and therefore everything needs a partner to help complete it. Only God is perfect and is the one and only being not needing any help.

Birthpangs

Just as a woman, feeling her birthpangs during childbirth, knows that this is merely a preparation for the blessed event, so too those who suffer know that it is for the good.

The Voice of Mitzvah

Every *mitzvah* has a voice and speaks to a particular part of the body. The more one desires to hear the message, the more he is able to connect to the depth of the *mitzvah*.

The Foundation

Each *mitzvah* is represented by a part of the human body. The vital organs symbolize the vital commandments. Thus the heels, the lowest part of the body, symbolize the smallest and easiest commandments. But the heels are also the foundation of the body, just like the small *mitzvos*, without which a person cannot stand erect.

High Feelings

The essence of observing a commandment is completing it to
its last detail. It is not the high feeling one may have as he
undertakes the *mitzvah*. Because if he does have a feeling of
conceit as he begins its observance, it is better if he were not
to do it at all.

Thoughts of Fear

The Jewish people have to take careful note of the thoughts
that pass through their hearts. And if by chance they enter-
tain a thought of fear, they should not think, "Oh, I have fear
in my heart; therefore I had better be afraid." No, not so! A
thought of fear should remind us of the mortal danger, during
the Exodus, from which God saved us totally and completely.
And He will do so now, too.

No Compromises

There are no compromises. If one accepts the yoke of heaven
in all his activities, sacrificing his life for the one and only God,
then blessing will follow. If not, curse. The Torah is in the world
before man's birth and is more precious than his entry into it.
It is imperative that he place the importance of the Torah
ahead of anything regarding his affairs.

Residue

Wherever holiness comes to rest, there remains a residue of holiness that is detectible and has influence forever.

Beginnings

At the onset of each day the world receives a spirit of purity, and so does each individual. Lurking and ready to pounce is evil, to balance that spirit. Therefore, whenever anything is starting—the onset of the day, the week, month or year, a new project or event—one must quickly seize the purity being offered before evil misleads him. Then, even if one stumbles into sin, the energy of that beginning will give him strength and hope.

Life in Eden

True joy is in the Garden of Eden, and, yes, it is in our life and is revealed to the servants of God.

Smart Eyes

Man has two types of eyes. He has the eyes of flesh and blood that see only what pleases the senses. Then there are the spiritual eyes, from his inner wisdom, the smart eyes. One should protect his smart eyes against all sensual bribery, lest they be blinded, unable to see right and wrong.

Battle

Because of man's sins he has to battle to observe each commandment and to pray with a pure heart. And because he battles the evil within, he will merit a complete repentance and purity of heart.

Continue

When a gate opens to see and understand God, we must continue. One gate leads to the next, endlessly, till we find every feeling and thought standing before God.

No Prejudices

If we are indeed witnesses we should cleanse our heart of any prejudice. And being God's witnesses, we must surely clear out all prejudice, favoring ourselves and our self-interests, from our life. Then our life is witness that God is the one and only king and ruler.

No Magic

The nation of God does not look for miracles, nor does it go to sorcerers to discover secrets. Rather, it works hard to purify its nature and raise it to the level of the soul. And with that it attains the highest spiritual insights.

Victory

Just as the nations prepare themselves for war with physical weapons and strategies, so too the Jewish people prepare themselves with spiritual connectedness to God. And therefore those who had spiritual lapses were not able to participate in the nation's wars. Even if they repented each and every time, war requires purity of heart of a different sort. In war one must continue non-stop till its conclusion, till victory. Unlike ordinary life, where mistakes are corrected and one who is lost can return to the desired path, in war the plan is not to err but to follow through to the end.

Little Good

Although no one can hope to fix all his deeds, still there is no Jew without good deeds. And that little bit must be protected in its purity. And that little will give him the spiritual strength needed to accomplish greater things.

One Mouth

You have two eyes, two ears, two nostrils, and one mouth. Doesn't that tell you how much more you should watch what you say?!

Sifting

One who is careful of the words he utters can utter amazing words; one who is careful of his deeds can accomplish great things. By choosing and sifting, only the best comes out, with little chaff. Similarly, God heals by bringing near, and by placing one far away.

Pure Vessel

One must take care not to block the flow of spiritual light from reaching his every organ. By observing all the negative commandments, one keeps the body as a vessel to receive the light of God.

Two Covenants

The Jewish people have two covenants with God that need to be watched very carefully. One is that God chose us and liberated us from Egyptian slavery, and we chose Him at Mount Sinai and accepted the Torah. That is the covenant of the mouth: prayer and Torah study. Both are signs that we are God's servants. The other covenant is circumcision, that we commit our children, without exception, to follow the path of God. That is a sign that we are children of God, and we want our children to be the same.

No Two Days Alike

There are 365 days in the year, each receiving its light from one of the 365 negative commandments, corresponding to the 365 sinews sustaining the organs of the body. God too, renews the universe each day and illuminates the world with a new light. Thus, there is a new image of the world each day that man has to perceive. (Things change all the time and quickly; they change for the worse in twenty-one days, as from Tamuz 17 to Av 9, the period of yearly mourning, and change for the good from Rosh Hashanah till Hoshanah Rabah, the period of rejoicing also twenty-one days.)

Washing the Soul

Repentance is not necessarily for sin only, but also to return to the roots. Therefore it reaches to God's throne of honor, that is, the soul of man that is connected to the most high. If we reveal God's throne on earth, He will reveal the hidden place of our soul, connected to His throne.

Difficult Challenges

You would think that the higher one rises in spirituality the easier it becomes. But this is not so. Each new level comes with more and more difficult challenges.

Means and Ends

A leaf helps the tree grow, minerals feed the plants, plants
are eaten by animals and finally eaten by man. One seems to
be the means, the other, the end. In the infinite light of God,
where there is no past or future, the divine dwells in the means
just as in the end. Similarly, any one letter of the Torah is not
only the means to form a word in the Torah; it contains the
entire Torah.

9

Desire

God's Will

When we do God's will with great joy even before we appreciate its wisdom, then God, too, allows His will to include our will.

Home

In order to reach the home of his soul, man needs to yearn for the highest spheres. Yet he should be equally happy in the physical home God has chosen for him. And this dilemma makes him swing back and forth between two places: being happy where he is, and yearning to be back home.

Cravings

Two of man's strongest cravings are to communicate and to procreate. And he can cleave to God with both of them. He can use his physical lust to beget children who reveal God's kingdom. And with his craving for communication he can express his total helplessness before God.

Shining Brightly

Silver cannot shine with its natural luster while it contains dross, and neither can man shine with yearning that pulls him toward the material world. But as that dross is removed, he shines once more.

High or Low?

The physical world seems to be the lowest of all the spheres, yet it is the one that God desired most. It is His greatest pleasure to watch as his noble creatures abandon the world's vanities and cleave to the divine within nature.

Desires

There really is no greater desire and yearning than for knowledge, the knowledge of the Torah. Our physical desires, however, eclipse our desire for the holy. What can be done? When we exert and immerse ourselves in Torah study, our desires for the holy become revealed.

One Desire

In any deed there should not be two desires, one's own and God's. One's sole desire should be that God's will is done.

Ultimate Truth

God's omniscience is the ultimate truth in the entire creation. Every creature yearns to be included in that truth. The more man reveals it, the more the creation is under his control.

Desiring Spirit

When doing a *mitzvah* one should focus all his desires on completing the will of God. Thus, even if one has other desires, the holy desire will predominate.

Choosing Desire

We can appreciate the more physical desires. It is only because we have many desires that we are able to choose from among them and serve God. And when we do, we raise even the wrong desires to a higher spiritual level.

True Desire

When one observes God's commandments, he ought to do only as much as his true desire. Whatever he does in addition will not last, as it is not part of his life. And because his deeds were full of true desire, God, too, will reward him and allow him to receive as much blessing as God desires to give him.

Prepare

God gives us the energy to observe His commandments. Then what is our contribution? We add the desire and preparation for the *mitzvah*.

Uplifted

Just as man's mouth reveals his desires, so too the desires of the entire creation are lifted up through the Jewish people.

One Mitzvah

All the 613 Torah commandments are in each one of the commandments. When one fulfills a commandment with *every* good intention and *every* type of perfection, it is as if he fulfilled the entire Torah.

Turn to God

One ought not to be impressed with what he sees. He ought to turn to God's commandments, the divine vitality in everything. And if he feels tainted by sin or inferior to the task of doing a *mitzvah*, God will surely help him complete it. After all, God is with him, and the mere fact that he is alive is positive proof of that.

Impossible

If one subordinates his logic to God's will, then even if his accomplishment is logically and statistically impossible, it becomes possible.

What You See

If one looks only to see and listens only to hear the godly in each thing, then it is revealed to him.

Logic

It is easier to do a *mitzvah* for God's sake when it is not logically understood. If it were understood, one would do it merely for its logic. One ought to look for the will of God in each creation and in each *mitzvah*.

Going Home

By remembering his dying day, man subordinates his physical desires to the soul. He also remembers that his soul, although descended from the upper spheres, will one day return there.

Quickness

Those who negate all their desires in order to do the will of God are blessed with quickness, doing God's service without the slightest delay.

Reward

One who is totally devoted to God is ready to give all his possessions and even his very life for God's sake. Certainly he does expect a reward!

As One's Rising

The nature of the day depends on one's manner of rising in the morning. Does he roar with vigor as he rises, like a lion, pushing aside all desires, so as to do only God's desire? Or is everything else more important to him? Similarly, the long history of the Jewish people follows their devoted commitment to God's service as they ran from Egypt and headed to Mount Sinai to accept the Torah.

Ready to Die for

The Torah will be found only by those who are ready to sacrifice everything for her. On the other hand, the Torah was given for life and not for death. Isn't this contradictory?

One needn't endanger his life except for three commandments: idol worship, forbidden relations, and murder. But with regard to the rest of the Torah's commandments, if one is ready to risk all for them, then he will merit not having to die for them.

An Animal

Logically, more wisdom is better than less. Yet animals serve their masters directly, while man is circumspect. To correct this, man must first be like an animal, serving God as a creature. Then he can rise to the level of man.

Evil Prosecutors

Just as the Jewish people overpower their desires for evil and persevere to do only God's will, so too God, so to speak, overpowers the evil prosecutors of the Jewish people and gives the Jewish people the power to bless and heal all of mankind.

The Rest of Nature

The way man decides to live his life, from head to toe, is the way nature will follow right behind. If man's thoughts are only of God and His kingdom, his speech and actions all focused on his creator, the rest of nature follows.

What to Hear

"Hear O Israel, God our God, God is the one and only!" Each and every day of a person's life he has what to hear and listen to. He must merely prepare his ears and heart to hear it.

He Reflected Them

Not only did the Jewish people long to receive the Torah, but God also desired to give it to them. Whatever they experienced was a mirror image of what God was doing for them. They neared Mount Sinai and so did He. Their souls left them when He spoke, and God, too, gave His whole Being with the Torah.

Invent Ways

Man must invent ways and work with heart and soul to find God's kingdom.

The Eye of the Needle

Man's every good deed is made possible by the Creator. God's control is like the shaft of a needle, and the eye of the needle is the part in our control. That eye is the awe of God that man chooses to have or not to have. And although tiny, it is the opening through which the rest of our life descends from heaven.

Return of Gifts

God plants man's every good deed, and therefore God desires the return of every gift He gives to man. While it is in the hands of the divine it is safe and sound. In the hands of man, what will happen to it?

New Reasons

The reasons for the Torah's commandments are infinite. And he who wants to do more and more good deeds will find a new reason each and every day.

Turning away Desire

Man has a physical body and a spiritual soul. His body has physical desires, and the Israelites gave up all of them at Mount Sinai to receive the Ten Commandments. In response, so to speak, God gives up the vastness of the universe, His desire, and dwells among them.

Giving up Desire

Our desires are stimulated by the crust of earthly creations.
That material part is limited, and we experience a tightness
and a blockage. That limitation is an illusion; really it is a challenge. If we give up our desire, on the other hand, and tune
in to God's desire, we experience boundless and infinite space.
That is the inner nature, the core of all things.

Like a Mother

Just as a mother waits to hear the sound of her child returning from school, so too we must always be ready to listen to
the word of God from wherever it might come.

To Hear

In the beginning, each day God created another creation.
Finally, when man was created and the entire creation was
complete, man was ready to listen to the word of God. He
was created as a vessel; his essence is to hear and to be tuned
in. Therefore, if one attacks another and causes his loss of
hearing, he must pay his full value.

Hunger and Thirst

The appetites of the body are the shadows of the soul's desires. They urge the body to partake of the world, to redeem the holy sparks within the food and drink and other pleasures. Those sparks are food for the soul. But there will come a day when the hidden will be revealed; when the Messiah comes, the hunger will no longer be for bread, and the thirst will not be for water but for hearing the word of God.

Judgment and Kindness

The world cannot exist with God's judgment alone. It is not perfect and would be judged unfit to exist. It therefore always needs His mercy and loving kindness. Thus, if man actively judges his every action, the heavenly response is kindness. The witnesses especially need to be questioned; they are the two desires of good and evil. Each one testifies that his way is correct. And when we question them, with patience and calm, without rushing to act, we produce judgment on earth deserving a response of kindness from God.

More Truth

If we attain even a small bit of truth, we should use it to get more and more truth.

No Weakness

Man's heart is weak and vulnerable only to the extent that he did not reconcile his two desires of good and evil. But he who has harnessed his every desire to the service of God experiences no weakness or fright of even the worst circumstance.

Listening

"Hear O Israel, God our Lord, God is the One and only!" The strength of the Jewish people lies in their listening carefully. They no longer have the merit of doing and observing. They have sinned. But by listening, which is still in its pristine purity, they can prevail.

Hard or Easy

Why is it that the hardest commandment to observe—honoring one's father and mother—has the same reward as the easiest commandment, for example, sending away a mother bird before taking her eggs? It is because the more difficult a commandment, the more power God gives to those who are trying to observe it. Therefore, although one seems hard and the other easy, they both may be just as easy to observe.

Like an Illusion

Man's desires are impermanent and are therefore like an illusion. They are therefore called the *yetzer hora* and *yetzer hatov*, the evil and good urges; *yetzer* also means illusion, as in *tziyur*. The soul of man, on the other hand, is permanent and can discern the truth.

Charming

"God saw all that He created and it was very good." The charm that the creation has is from that original look and the satisfaction that God felt about the creation. Therefore those who observe God's commandments include themselves in that original charm, the creation that followed God's command.

Similarly, every part of man's body, by doing a *mitzvah*, is witness that it was created for the sole purpose of doing God's will, just like the original creation. And one who possesses this charm will be helped through any difficulty.

The Charm of Evil

Each and every thing exists because God desires it. Even evil must have some charm, some part of it that God desires; otherwise it could not exist. And that desirable portion is found when one overcomes the evil desire. At that moment man needs great protection, because the part of the evil that finds favor in God's eyes is now released from captivity with an irresistible charm.

Divine Desire

God desires the Jewish people, and therefore they exist eter-
nally. By observing the commandments we connect to that
desire. No matter whether it is the hardest or the easiest commandment, it connects us just as strongly.

Difficult Task

God desires that the Jewish people fix their hearts, each composed of two hearts, just as the tree of knowledge, composed
of good and evil. Therefore their life is always considered a
mixture and their task a difficult one.

Distractions

The world is full of distractions, both outside and inside our
body. We need to focus all our energies on listening, and then
we can hear the word of God.

Our Share

Nothing gets completed without God's help. Thus all our good deeds and any accomplishments are rightfully credited to God. Still, man also has a small share in it, his yearning to observe the Torah. And that is the reward of a *mitzvah*: God helps you do the *mitzvah* as a reward for your desire. Similarly, when parents desire that their children follow the Torah's path, God shines its light into the hearts of those children. Also, when even the plainest people subordinate themselves to a *tzadik*, a righteous person, it begets good desires in their hearts.

One who has a noble desire ought not to wait till someone comes along to join him in his good deed. He should immediately share his enthusiasm for the *mitzvah* with others, because it is certainly more noble for a whole group to do a good deed than for only one person to do it!

Risking All

To risk one's own life for a *mitzvah* is to negate his desires, even the desire to rise higher spiritually. One is then a vessel for God's will.

Abraham's Spirit

Abraham negated his desires so as to do the will of God. And those who possess the three qualities of a generous eye, a humble spirit, and a meek soul are his students, imbued with his spirit of total devotion.

Longing to Yearn

Angels are always ready to do God's will. On the other hand, people are not that loyal. The most we can do is yearn to be always yearning to do God's will. And with our heart open and ready, God grants us great spiritual revelations from time to time, unexpected and undeserved.

10

Kindness

True Joy

The world was created so that God's kingdom is recognized through His deeds. And when God helps an individual or a people, they should rejoice with His kingdom that was revealed. What joy!

Giving

The hand is the vessel both for giving and for receiving. One who gives everything away to God's will receives everything in return.

Kindness

One who is constantly seeking to do acts of kindness will look for kindness in everything that happens.

Wholeness

No human being could ever finish anything on his own without God, Who is the King of wholeness and completeness.

First and Last

First, God, mercifully offers everyone a path leading to His service. The choice is in their hands to work and arrive there by their own merit. And when one arrives, God tells him, "I am first, and I am last; I started you off and I help you finish!"

Deserving

The world survives only because of divine kindness, and only with kindness can one succeed. There are those who would never receive kindness unless they deserved it, and even that is kindness.

Ready to Give

One who is ready to give his life away to serve God is deserving of God's kindness.

Perfect Plan

Action is always imperfect, although the intention, the plan, is a perfect one. Yet if someone is ready to risk his life to accomplish the deed, God helps him finish it according to plan.

From Your Mouth

We ask God, "Please don't put food on our plate. Give it to us straight from Your mouth, like two lips kissing; give us life from the fountain of life."

Constantly Looking

God, Who sees the entire creation at a glance, sees that it is very good. And He is constantly looking at it, and that is divine providence.

Energy of Sin

How can there be sin in the world? Where is the source of its energy? The source is repentance; in the end some good will come out of it. Just think, without repentance, you would not even have the energy to sin.

In Sickness Itself

Who can understand God's ways? There are many medicines hidden in nature, and sometimes in the sickness itself, the *bitter* is cured with the *bitter*. Still, man has to look for the word of God in everything.

Sharing Gifts

It is not a feat to be intelligent; that is a divine gift. The task is what to do with God's gifts. And if one chooses to share his gifts constantly with others, his deeds are always ahead of his wisdom and make his wisdom grow even more.

Peace to All

Quarreling is destructive even to those who normally are not involved. And it is even more true of peacemaking that it brings near even those who are not worthy.

The Law

There are spiritual laws of retribution, and also God's mercy. One of these laws is that by giving one tenth of your produce to the poor, you will become rich. And since it is a law, one must do the exact measure.

Love Your Friend

The commentaries explain, "Love your neighbor as yourself," as referring to the love of God. Because he who loves God loves his friend, who loves God as he does. And thus the truth is revealed: loving your friend and God are one and the same.

Ability

Each human being is capable of being productive and earning a livelihood according to his talents and intelligence. And God grants him sustenance in that measure. But there is also providence from a place beyond nature, from where man receives more than his abilities merit.

Leniency

There are two sides to kindness and to strict judgment. When we exercise kindness, we must be wary of laxity in values. And when we sit in judgment, we must also be wary, lest it cause us to condemn unnecessarily. Therefore the laws of the Torah are concluded in favor of leniency.

Disunity

The universe before creation was in absolute unity, the virtue of loving kindness. In creation it spread and became more and more disunited, in strict judgment. The more judgment spreads, the more the world is in danger. The work of the righteous is to lift up the lower, disunited levels to the higher, united realm. And this has to be done constantly, because disunity is the nature of the world.

What Greatness!

One is fortunate if he recognizes the great gifts that he receives through the Torah. But one also has to realize that he really has no idea what greatness lies in the Torah.

Model

If one models his life according to the Torah's teachings, his life also will reflect God's will.

The Fiftieth Rung

Man can fall lower and lower on the rungs of the spiritual ladder, forty-nine levels toward defilement and evil. It is not humanly possible to overcome the challenge of the fiftieth rung of defilement. And only the mercy of God saves him.

Healing Tongue

Just as man's tongue can cause great harm and damage, it can cause even more good, healing, and blessing.

Virtue and Wisdom

All man's virtues, all his wisdom and his blessings, are nothing; but to receive the same from God, that's something!

More Faith

The fact that God carries us around is obscured because of the exile. Thus the deeper the exile, the more faith is needed.

Reproof and Blessing

If the Jewish people accept God's reprimands, He blesses them in return. Actually, the words of reproof are the same as those of the blessings.

Success

In life, results depend on the amount of work you put into a project. Not so with Torah. The Torah itself heals, raises, and makes successful those who diligently study and observe her commandments.

Heavenly Battle

The heavenly realm is a mirror image of the earthly realm. And if there is a great battle to observe the Torah on earth, then in heaven, too, God's mercy, so to speak, has to overpower the accusing voices of the evil nations.

Own Effort

The Torah is a gift inside your heart. The first door opens to a room filled with the awe of God and must be opened with one's own effort.

Each Day

Each day has its unique revelation, distinct opportunity, and particular venture. We need to immerse our deeds into those gifts and observe the commandments in a new way.

God Himself

God does not use angels as messengers to punish the Jewish people. He deals with them intimately and directly to remove the crust, the physical separation between man and God.

Open Your Heart

Any spiritual inspiration, no matter how deep or how shallow, is from God. And that inspiration should be the cause of our heart opening, even if only a tiny bit. How can we accomplish this difficult task? By being mindful, attentive, and aware. We should not fall into the habit of taking things for granted, but should notice the gifts we are receiving constantly. Then when our heart opens, and we feel inspired, we will be thankful, and our heart will open even more.

Honest Judgment

If each person judges himself internally and examines his guilt and innocence meticulously, and similarly, between man and man, each carefully judges the relationship between them, there is then judgment on earth, and God's mercy sustains the creation.

Compassion

Man has compassion for another human being because it is his own kind, and less compassion for animals because they are not his kind. He has empathy and feels the pain and suffering of those who are like him. Similarly, angels have no compassion for mankind. God, however, understands the being of every creature, and His compassion excludes no one.

Channel

When you do a *mitzvah* and create a channel for the spirit to descend and infuse your body, God has mercy on your body and shines His spirit into you.

Saved Reward

There are deeds that create blessing so sublime that one hasn't the vessels to receive it. God watches it, saves it for one, perhaps for the future or for the World to Come, when one will be prepared to receive it.

11

Choosing Good or Evil

Love and Lust

Although both the wicked and the righteous yearn and lust, they are two opposites. The lust of the wicked is for wrongful and sinful acts. Even after they commit their sin, their heart, rather than filling with love, is full of remorse and resentment. On the other hand, in the case of the *tzadikim*, who do acts of loving kindness with their love, their love merely increases and becomes even stronger.

In the Vestibule

The physical world is like a vestibule compared to the World to Come, which is like the palace. Still, man's struggle to learn Torah and observe the *mitzvos* in the vestibule is immensely more valuable in God's eyes than all the splendors of the palace. After all, in the vestibule he is charged with a divine mission, while in the palace he is merely collecting his reward.

Pure Silver

Just as the removal of the dross from silver purifies it, similarly, the purification gets rid of the dross. Pure silver purges dross. The repentance of sinners purifies the congregation, and the purification of the group causes the sinners to repent.

Unity and Discord

The higher one ascends into the spiritual spheres, the more unity he will find. On the lowest levels there is discord and chaos, and it is man's task, through hard work and perseverance, to sort the good from the evil, the light from the darkness.

Final Battle

The spiritual realm has two aspects; one is holiness, the other is evil that makes us abhor the good, especially God's commandments. Man will battle with evil all his life, each with his particular evil. And unfortunately, in a battle to the death, injuries are unavoidable. No one escapes without blemish.

Destiny

Man's food is a mixture of good and evil and is called bread of the earth, the Tree of Knowledge. Ideally, he would be nurtured by bread from heaven, the Tree of Life. But man must learn to separate good from evil in all aspects of his life. That is his destiny and task on earth.

A Shadow

The power of evil is an illusion, like a shadow, having no substance. And one who is brave enough to take up the battle against it finds nothing but a shadow. Those who fear it, however, are afraid of it as if it had great power and lurking danger.

Start and End

There are two paths: one is smooth in the beginning but rocky and crooked in the end. The other is first rocky, and then smooth in the end. Similarly, the nation of evil is full of evil as soon as they start. The Jewish people, on the other hand, start with goodness, get better and better, and move toward perfection.

Guarding the Divine

Just as it is important to seek holiness and divinity in the world, it is equally important to place a gate around it to guard it, so that it does not dissipate.

Constant Struggle

One should not be discouraged by his failings in serving God. It is the way of the world, a constant up-and-down movement, ascending and descending, war and peace, war and peace. There is really no place of rest but only a continuous struggle toward perfection.

Cursing the Good

The reason the wicked can curse is that the world is a mixture of good and evil. But the Torah is the Tree of Life, purely good, and all who hold on to it cannot be cursed.

On the Edge

Evil and wickedness follow holiness and stalk it on its edges and borders. Therefore those places always need extra protection.

The Mind of a Witness

To be a witness, one needs a clear mind to know what he is perceiving, so as to distinguish between good and evil. The Jewish people are witnesses to God's kingdom in all the three realms. In the realm of space, they witness with the Holy Temple. In the realm of time, they witness with the Sabbath. And in the realm of the soul, they themselves are the witnesses. All three realms must be free of evil in order to witness.

Wicked Humility

There are students of the good and students of wickedness. The wicked also humble themselves, but only to satisfy their lust. On the other hand, the righteous do everything only for God's sake, not for any reward.

From the Beginning

Although clearly separated, each with its own destiny, good and evil appear as a cloudy mixture, impossible to separate. Thus, although hidden from human eyes and comprehension, that which is given to the righteous and God's chosen had been there since the beginning.

Sweet Throughout

In the end the will of God will prevail; the crooked will be made straight, the bitter, sweet, the blind will see and the light of God's kingdom will pervade throughout. And the plans of the wicked to plunge the world into darkness will come to naught.

So Little

The inheritance of the Jewish people is the World to Come, while the present material world, the domain of the nations, is of little consequence to them. And because it is of so little significance, they are blessed with material good, too. Thus they have both worlds, the material and the spiritual.

Protect the Kernel

When man protects the divine kernel from defilement, then it is protected from the scheming of the wicked, too.

Sneaky Bowing

The wicked bow and bend down so they can sneak over and snatch blessings that do not belong to them. In the case of the righteous, however, whatever they do, their goal is to humble themselves before God.

Esau's Hands

When the hands of the Israelites are low, they resemble the hands of Esau, warring and quarrelsome. By raising the low hands to the higher, divine energy of the hands, the power of the wicked is overcome.

Genuine Rest

Every spiritual battle is followed by genuine rest and peace.

Connecting

The wicked have no problem with the heavens. What bothers them the most is the work of the righteous, who try to connect the earth to the heavens.

Purity

There is holiness, undefiled, clearly separated good from evil. And there is the lower level, purity, accomplished by purification. One reaches purity by first being impure, a mixture of good and evil. Holy men are connected to the essence of the Torah, the written Law. Those who are pure are connected to the oral Law.

The Wicked

When the heavenly doors open, even the wicked might be uplifted. But just then, to balance the opportunity, they are filled with hatred for anything good or holy. There are other times when the heavenly doors are closed, a weak opportunity to mend the ways of the wicked. And just then, to balance, the wicked are very friendly and accommodating. In either case, only the deepest Torah wisdom can guide one to decide what to do.

Bitter and Sweet

The natural and the spiritual worlds are opposites. There is bitterness in the world of nature. Although one lusts and indulges, he later feels jaded as his lusts far outdistance his attainment. On the other hand, the spiritual is sweet. And one who observes the Torah's commandments, although he has no great desire, will get an appetite for the spiritual afterward.

Lofty Emotions

Lust and desire are lofty emotions that can be catalysts for
the achievement of higher levels of spirit. We must cherish
and respect them and not waste them on whims and impermanent pursuits.

Impurity

God created purity and impurity to show that impurity has no
independent power and always returns to purity.

Heart United

Man's heart and desires lean in two directions, good and evil.
When he accepts the Torah as his life's guide, both desires
unite to serve God. This was true at Mount Sinai for the Jewish nation as a whole, and it is true even today.

Challenges

The *yetzer hora*, the inclination to evil, at its root is actually
good. It is there to challenge man to do better. And the better
he does the more he needs to be challenged . . . by the *yetzer
hora*.

The Door Is Open

The door is open for any soul, lost in the mire of evil, that desires to join the body of *klal Yisroel*, the Jewish congregation.

Sinner's Challenge

The *yetzer hora*, the evil inclination, challenges man at every twist and turn. Thus, when one's deeds put him far from God, and he wishes to be near, the *yetzer hora* argues that it is not fitting for a sinner to feel close to God. And that itself is a challenge.

Weaker and Weaker

Each generation, because of its distance from the Mount Sinai experience and the increasing challenge from the length of the exile, gets spiritually weaker and weaker. Thus, if we but sin unintentionally, down the line our descendants may sin intentionally.

The Power of Evil

The more developed one is spiritually, the more he is challenged by the *yetzer hora*, the inclination to evil. How can he ever win? If he subordinates himself to God, and is like dust and ashes before Him, no evil can have power over him.

Edifices of Folly

Just as the wise build the spiritual edifice of the world with the letters of the Torah, the wicked, in contrast, build their edifices of vanity, folly, and nonsense. Those structures must be demolished before the spiritually healthy challenges are built.

Blessings and Curses

The righteous demand and reprimand, then, in the end, bless and praise; the wicked, on the other hand, first bless and praise, but end with curses and condemnation.

Husk

The paper-thin husk has body and shape while it covers the wheat kernel. Once the wheat is removed, it is but husk, a wisp of straw blown away by wind. Similarly, all wickedness has substance only as long as the kernel of goodness is within.

The Crooked Are Straight

God rules over all and plots the path for His creatures. All the paths that seem crooked, the most obscure and impassable ones, are really straight in the divine plan.

Beyond

There are two obstacles to understanding the spiritual realm. It is very deep and beyond us; moreover, evil gets in the way. God in His great mercy opens the heavens for us; they are not beyond our reach. He also removes evil from the path of our understanding.

Balance

The world is in balance between good and evil. And if the Jewish people righteously observe the Torah, the evil of the wicked really stands out. Otherwise, one is not so much worse than the other.

Dependent

The livelihood of other creatures may not be tied to their deeds. For the Jewish people it is so. Their responsibilities are so serious that even earthly comforts are tied to their observance of the Torah's commandments. If they observe the commandments they have rain, and if not, there is a lack thereof.

Soft and Hard

The heart is soft and full of mercy and kindness, and to balance it there is the sheath covering the heart, callousness and heartlessness. The head contains the soul and all its intelligence, and also the stiff-necked animal stubborness bordering on ignorance. They are balanced perfectly, so that man can choose one or the other.

Planted

God planted the ability to differentiate between good and evil, and to choose the blessing, into every Jewish heart. And with every commandment, this ability becomes renewed and its strength energized.

Negative Energy

Every material creation is surrounded with the negative energy of hiding God's kingdom. We must break through that shell with our strong desire to connect to the spirit within.

Choosing Again

Each and every day of his life, man is free to choose life or death, blessing or curse. And even if one chose the path of the wicked, and allowed his heart to slip into evil, he can choose again.

Habits

How can one hope to get rid of a bad habit or evil urge? First dilute it and overwhelm it with good deeds. And most important, uproot it so that no residue of it remains, which is impossible without God's help.

Man's Goal

The goal of man is not to better himself and rise higher and higher in spiritual levels. Rather, it is to do away with the root of evil completely, and to enhance the root of good.

Choices

Regardless of how righteous one's goals, intentions, and actions, or how wicked, there are forever and always two paths before every human being.

'Evil 'Urge

On the day of judgment, when God will do away with the evil urge, both the righteous and the wicked will be there to watch. Both will cry. To the righteous the urge will appear as a mountain, and to the wicked as a strand of hair. The righteous will cry, "How were we ever able to conquer that mountain?" while the wicked will moan, "Why were we not able to overcome a strand of hair?!"

The truth is that the evil urge is a strand of hair that the righteous overcome one at a time, thousands of times, over and over in their lives. Thus the vanquished urges pile up to the size of a mountain. The wicked, on the other hand, never overcame their first strand of hair, and there it still is in front of them!

Always the Crossroads

Man is always at a crossroads. In one direction is a path full of thorns and hardship, ending smoothly. In the other direction is another path, smooth but ending with thorns.

The Torah constantly creates that crossroads so that anyone can get off the wicked path if they choose to. One can choose the path of life. It will be hard, filled with thorns, but well worth it, ending smoothly.

All the Evil

When the evil urge approaches, one must not have any compassion toward it. It must be immediately and completely terminated. And with that, the power of evil is weakened, not only for oneself, but for anyone who meets up with it. Thus the struggle is not for the individual, but for the entire Jewish nation and all of mankind.

Admixture

Every light and illumination from heaven is accompanied by darkness and evil. There is always an admixture of good and evil, and always a choice: death or life? And you shall choose life!

Root of all Gates

Every door that opens, even in man's heart, has the possibility of forty-nine aspects of good and forty-nine aspects of evil. And if man, upon hearing all the gates clamoring for their roots, negates himself to the fiftieth gate, the root of all gates, where all is unity, he is then with God.

Simple Desire

What is man to do with every particle of his being, with good and evil quarreling for supremacy? He must negate all his desires leaning one way or the other and cleave to the simple, unified desire of God.

Within You

When evil seems stronger, lust more attractive, wickedness more glorified, it is from within you. It is an illusion caused by your weak heart and spirit. And if the enemy appears to you, you must possess the spiritual energy, hidden inside, to fight and overcome it.

Move and Run

Only one of the Torah's commandments asks us to move far away from evil: the commandment to move away from falsehood. As much as we move away from it, this is not nearly enough. And to seek truth, we must run. In a world of lies and deceit, one will never reach truth by walking.

Silliness

When man gathers all his desires and is ready to sacrifice all of them for God's honor, no wicked silliness can entice him.

Breaking Desire

How is the power of the evil desire broken? By thinking: if it were permissible, would I be doing it? And if it is permissible, who needs it?

Small Deeds

How does the evil urge overwhelm man with evil? It entices man to transgress with small sins, time and time again. The cumulative effect is devastating. The repentance is to appreciate each and every good deed, even the smallest, and protect it from defilement.

Battle Together

One needs to join the nation of Israel in their battle against evil and hope for their success. Then he too will have strength against his own temptations.

Leaving Evil

Once man decides to leave his evil ways behind, even if he finds this too difficult to do, he is helped by God to complete his heart's desire.

Giving Life

If the mouth can be used to give life, as in mouth-to-mouth resuscitation, or healing words, can you imagine how terrible it is to use it for evil, as in slander and defamation?!

With Light

When man is ready to battle with his evil urge, the spiritual light within every part of his body is revealed to him, and he is better able to vanquish the enemy.

At the Door

Whenever a door opens for the light of God to enter, there evil lurks and tries also to enter. Therefore every opening of one's heart needs protection with humility, realizing that one is merely at the door and is a beggar. One is nothing yet, and perhaps with the grace of God one will become something.

The symbol for door is the letter *dalet*, the fourth letter of the Hebrew alphabet. When we place a *yod*, the tiniest letter, inside the *dalet* it becomes a *heh*, the fifth letter. God's name is spelled, *Yod*, then *heh*, and *vov*, and *heh*. The *heh* has a *yod* inside a *dalet*, a small *mezuzah* to guard the door from evil. And if we are already at the door, we should proceed to open the next door, to continue rising and developing in spirit and not get stuck at the door.

Head and Hands

The hands, physical power, can revert to deeds of violence and wickedness. Therefore the hands are situated and bent so that they constantly move toward the head. This alludes to the raising of the physical powers to those of the soul in our head.

Food and Joy

Wickedness and evil is the chaff on the grain and should be removed. And if it is, instead of sadness, joy, instead of chaff, food.

With Fire

Every human being has a share in the quality called *beginning*. But alas, who can benefit from it when it is sunken into materialistic pursuits and sucked up by the wicked? But he who connects to the inner beginning, the root and origin, remembers what is important. Like a lamp with its flame rising on its own, so too is the *mitzvah* done with fervor, the fire of love and faith.

Doors

There are heavenly doors through which divine providence descends to the earth, and there are earthly doors that man opens to receive God's gifts. Both are necessary for life to go on.

Heaven and Earth

With our good deeds we draw the heavenly wholeness into nature. With that the creation rises to become one with God.

12

Prayer

Call to God

Even in the darkest, most dire circumstances, one can call out to God, and He is there, no matter how distant one feels from Him.

Only Prayer

Even when we lift our hands to defend life and the holy, they are hands lifted in prayer. Only those will succeed.

Man-Made Vessels

The waters of a *mikvah* (ritual bath) should not be brought in a man-made vessel. Similarly, the providence we pray for is not the stuff of the earth but the infinite waters from the heavenly brook.

Fear of Danger

When one is filled with awe of God as the one and only, master of all events, he can then be told to fear nothing else. On the other hand, if he fears consequences and dangers, how could he be told to ignore them?

———

Response to Prayer

When we pray we stand before God face to face. The response to prayer is Torah, wherein God stands before us face to face.

———

Divine Dialogue

There is an ongoing dialogue between God and man, and God and the Jewish people. Our part of the dialogue is our words of prayer and Torah study. And just as divine acts are simultaneous with His command, our acts of charity must also precede our words.

———

God's Honor

The sum total of the creation is to bring honor to God, and all honor originates in the Torah. From each creature we can learn to honor God, and it is their song of praise to Him.

Undeserving Creature

Can we ever ask God for anything as if we earned it? If we earned it, why don't we have it? Obviously, it is a gift. By standing before God as a totally undeserving creature, we are able to ask and receive.

Prayer and Repentance

There is a place in man's heart where the holy spark is found. And to pray, he needs to subordinate and focus all his desires to that spark. Repentance is different. Man turns to face God and subordinates his being to His. He looks upward and seeks to ascend to a higher level.

Realizing

In prayer man moves from his place and brings himself closer to God. There he suddenly realizes that he and his entire life originate from God. Everything starts with Him, and without Him nothing would be.

The Power of Prayer

The question is: if God's judgment brought the need or suffering to man, how will it change because of prayer? Is he not praying to God, Who had decreed the calamity to come upon him? Yes, God decreed. Yet He also decreed that those who turn to Him for help can change the decree and thus be helped and saved.

Prayer

Prayer is faith, and faith is prayer.

The Royal Family

Those who pay homage to the king do not cease to praise Him, while the royal family acknowledges Him quietly. Similarly, the holy sparks hidden in every creation praise God in silence.

Ageless

Nature is framed in space and time and gets older and older. But God created it, and He does not age. Man, through his prayers, helps to connect nature to its creator, the aging to the ageless.

Affirming

All *mitzvos* and good deeds are really a prayer affirming the kingdom of God.

Final Touch

In the physical world nothing is perfect and nothing can be complete. The one small part missing and incomplete is waiting for God's mercy to make it whole. And for that final touch man prays.

Head and Tail

The root and "head" of everything is in the spiritual realm. The manifest part of it, the material portion, is the "tail." Our prayer is always to be connected to the "head" and not to the "tail end" of life. The "head" combines the entire world of spirit, and the "tail" combines all of material existence. Thus the righteous have power with the spiritual, while the wicked rule with physical energies.

Power of Speech

Man's ability to speak differentiates him from all other creatures. Therefore the speech, sounds, and breath that come from deep inside him need great protection. And they are protected by the commandment to speak words of Torah, to utter prayerful words, healing and loving speech. And most of all, even if one cannot compose and utter the proper words before God, he should nevertheless not utter anything improper.

Primal Scream

Man's prayers are limited to the words that he uses. But if he is speechless, wanting to call out to God with all his strength, his entire mind and heart, but cannot, that call is heard from one end of the universe to the other. It is similar to the scream of the soul as it leaves the body in death. The scream that is not uttered resonates in all creatures who also possess a great desire to call out to God.

Call for Help

Do not say, "I had no choice!" as long as you can call out to God for help. Do not allow evil to sway you or to have power over you. Cry out to God, plead and beg that you should be saved from the clutches of evil. Then you will see how the power of evil is broken and its grip loosens from around your throat.

Words to Live By

What one utters and verbalizes has an influence on one. Therefore, each day let us clearly state that we want to pray with all our heart and study the Torah with diligence. Those two activities will break the power of evil.

Guarded Words

A slave has nothing to say. When one is liberated he regains the power of speech. That privilege must be guarded to the utmost lest it be defiled or used for evil. Words uttered from a guarded mouth have influence and can sway our life to observe the Torah and its commandments.

Great Wonder

The greatest wonder is that man can speak and can choose what he will do. For the wicked, however, it would be better had if they neither spoken nor chosen.

Revitalized

The positive commandments open one's mouth, which is the source for the soul's revitalization with prayer and Torah study. The negative commandments are to guard the soul's energy from being used for evil.

In Place

Man's joy comes from being connected to his roots with his thoughts and emotions in order and in their place. And that is accomplished by prayer before each and every activity and change.

Yearning to Pray

Although there are set times for the three prayers of the day—
morning, afternoon, and night—the desire and yearning for
prayer must be with you all day long, every moment. That is
the door that we must open, and in response God opens the
doors of the heavens to listen to our prayers.

Morning of Life

We pray three times a day; in the morning, we pray to thank
God for our life; in the afternoon, we humble and prostrate
ourselves even more; in the evening, we must completely subordinate and humble our being to God. Similarly, in the morning of life when we are young, we pray to humble ourselves
and thank God for His kindness; later, in maturity, we pray to
change most of our deeds for the better; and with old age, we
pray to completely transform our deeds and subordinate ourselves to God. We are therefore called *zaken*, an acrostic for
ze shekana chochmo, he who has earned wisdom, because
at that stage all we want is to bask in the wisdom of God,
knowing that all else is vanity.

Standing with Strength

If one is not renewed he withers and droops. He is without strength and cannot stand. With renewal, one regains his strength and can stand erect, even stand before God. He who stands firmly, observing God's commandments, as if at Mount Sinai and receiving the Torah, can then stand before God in prayer. Prayer contains eighteen blessings, one for each of the vertebrae, setting them erect to stand before the Creator.

Night of Pain

When one is in trouble, suffering, and pain, his call to God from the deepest depths is heard on high more than any other time. And that is the essence of the evening prayer.

All about Him

The essence of prayer is to affirm, to praise God: He has the power to help and save all who need Him. And even if you are praying because you need help, it should be only about Him and not about your need. Your need will be fulfilled because it brought you to pray and praise God for His power of help.

13

Love of God

Awesome Closeness

God is different from a king of flesh and blood. Those closer to the king, able to observe his human nature, are less in awe of him than those further away. Not so with man's relating to God. The closer one is, the more one is in awe of Him.

God's Honor

Does man, who is a zero compared to God, have power to effect His honor? He does, but only adversely. If man is arrogant, God's holy presence leaves. Thus by humbling oneself, one causes people to recognize God's greatness.

Not a Thing

The lust of the wicked is dependent on the object of their desire. It is there because they desire the object. The desire of the righteous, on the other hand, is to be close to God, and they want nothing from it. Their desire for His awesome presence drives them.

From a Distance

God is awesome, and while some can stand near to fully appreciate His greatness, others can do so only from a distance. It is true wisdom to know one's place, and there is a constant balance between the two opposites.

Always in Prayer

Because the Jewish people wish to be close to God, they find any excuse to pray and bless, to praise and beseech.

Discover God

The world that God knows has no darkness and is full of light. He knows everything about Himself and there is nothing to discover. Then how can a creature honor God? By discovering His kingdom and light with his own efforts.

Infinite Light

Light that man brings into the world through his good deeds is limited. It is his task to connect his light to God's light, to cause his light to be infinite, too.

Minuscule

The greatest test for man is that, although he is aware of God's infinite kingdom, and his deeds seem so minuscule and insignificant, he still does God's commandments.

Consumed

Man must follow the path God chose for him, not as surrender, but as love, knowing how good it is. One ought to be filled with such intense desire and enthusiasm for the will of God that any self-centered desire is consumed by the fire of the spirit.

Turbulent Waters

The vanities of the world are like turbulent waters, and our tenacity in clinging to God is the ship.

Like an Angel

An angel's entire existence is his mission: to fulfill God's command. And if a human being can match such determination, completely ignoring all self-interest, he will succeed.

Riches

Riches will never amount to anything unless received as a gift from God. When viewing something as a gift, one realizes that it has a source, and one seeks and finds it.

Conviction

With its beauty and delight for the senses, the material world is attractive. Thus we strive for the spiritual, not because of boredom and disgust with the material world, but out of conviction that the greatest good is to be near God with a pure and empty heart.

A Little Success

Although it is an impossible task, man ought to be so committed to God's will that he never forgets it for an instant. And because of his lofty intentions, he will succeed to some degree.

Three Qualities

To love God you must have three qualities: a generous eye, a humble spirit, and a meek soul. Each is another way to humble oneself before God: to look at others and be happy for what God gave them; to negate all physical, as well as spiritual, accomplishments; and to be totally humble before God.

Repulsing Attacks

A reliable witness is one who can be challenged as to the day and time of the event in question, and can repulse every attack on his veracity. Similarly, those who are witnesses for God's kingdom are only as true as the attacks they are ready and willing to repulse.

Expecting Nothing

The Jewish people worship God without expecting a reward, and God, too, loves them without expecting anything.

Singing

The one who sings after a miracle occurs is connected to the miracle.

Great Miracles

The masses, who are intellectually unprepared, are awed by ordinary miracles. The spiritually developed man of God, knowing that God can do anything, is awed only by the greatest miracles. Still, not to cool the faith of the masses, he must join in their rejoicing even for the ordinary miracles.

Divine Togetherness

In the natural world all that is together falls apart. Therefore a gathering that is not for the sake of heaven will have just such an end. But if they gather for a divine purpose, the source of all unity, then their togetherness will last.

Near and Far

God is the furthest from mankind, and yet He could not be any closer. Some people, too, can reach completion from the closeness of God, while others reach it from His remoteness.

To See

The Hebrew word for seeing, yiro, and the word for awe have the same root. When one sees how God is in full control and guides the destiny of all, he is filled with awe.

Expert

People have a variety of occupations, and the more they repeat their occupation the more experienced and expert they become in it. Thus, if one is occupied with the awe of God, he becomes wiser and wiser in it, because his awe preceded his knowledge.

I Will Never Leave You

God's presence in us and around us is what keeps, protects, and consoles us in all difficulties and exiles. It is the Sinai experience and the beginning of all instruction of the Torah: "I am your God . . . ." I am with you and will never leave you.

Children of God

If we agree to be servants of God and to follow His teachings, we will be worthy to experience our true nature of being the children of God.

One Movement

One who is filled with knowledge of God serves Him with all his heart. But to get there from afar, one must approach with prayer. Thus prayer and Torah are two sides of one movement of man toward his Creator.

Always Ready

Man must observe the commandments but also be in a state of mind such that he is always ready to observe them.

God's Reprimands

When one realizes that the one who reprimanded him loves him loyally and unfailingly, he also trusts that the reprimand was for his benefit. And when man assumes this about God's reprimands, decrees, and exiles, although we suffer, they are reversed so that we experience what we believe.

Down and Up

Moses brought the Torah down to the Jewish people and brought their heart up to heaven.

Feelings from Heaven

One does not strike his finger on earth unless it was decreed in heaven. And neither does man feel any other pain, or any feeling for that matter, unless decreed. Therefore one ought to serve God with every one of those feelings. And that is the meaning of "You should serve God with all your heart."

Love Planted

The philosophers ask: how can man be commanded to love God? Isn't love an emotion that is either there or not there? And that is the answer; God planted love for Him into every heart; it is hidden and needs merely to be uncovered.

To Risk All

When God spoke the first word of the Ten Commandments on Mount Sinai, the souls of the Jewish people flew out of them. They realized that the same would happen again after each word. Yet they risked their lives to listen to the Ten Commandments, the Torah. How precious every utterance was to them! Similarly, we can never listen to God's words unless we are ready to risk all for it.

The Day Itself

On any day that one observes a *mitzvah*, the day itself comes before God and testifies on his behalf.

Must Sacrifice

Why did God's words at Mount Sinai cause the souls of the Israelites to depart? Why didn't God speak to them in a benign manner? It was a lesson for all time; no one can approach the Torah without sacrifice, without laying down one's very life for it.

Creatures

Man, as a creature, must praise God. Isn't that the purpose of his creation? Yet he is only a creature with limitations, and he prays to God to be able to do more. That is the essence of all prayer.

Life and Love

We are commanded to love God. Is love something that we can merely turn on and off? No, not in natural circumstances. But the Jewish people give away their entire life, are in a realm higher than nature, and connect to the love of God.

Inside and Outside

There are many loves and many things to love in a lifetime. They are all on the outside, while the love of God, one's Creator, is on the inside and is our very life.

Cause Us Love

Not only must we love God, but we must also love everything that causes us to love God, like the Torah and the commandments.

Friend of God

The king's friend causes him to befriend the entire kingdom. Similarly, if we are a friend of God, then God's friends increase; more people befriend Him.

God Will Help

Even if you do not have unflinching faith in God's help, still, do not be afraid. Remember all the times God helped in the past.

Love

Love is a feeling of kinship. By observing the commandments we imitate God and get to love Him.

Closer and Closer

The purpose of studying Torah and observing the commandments is to cleave to and get to love the Creator. The more frequently one accepts the yoke of the Torah, the closer he gets to the Creator.

Love Pains

What is the pain of divine love? It is when we experience pain and think, "God is reminding me to return to Him with all my heart." Thus the curses mentioned in the Torah are not meant to remain curses, but to turn to blessing when followed by repentance.

God's Love Within

Man must realize that his birth and being were made possible by the loving kindness of God. And for each thing and circumstance that comes his way, he has to connect to God's love in it. Even when he desires physical pleasures like eating and drinking, he should not for a moment forget God's love that brings him those gifts.

Receiving

God with His great love is constantly sustaining the world. The creatures must receive His sustenance, however. They must recognize that the Creator is giving and they are receiving. And they do, with the help of the Jewish people, who keep reminding them where their sustenance is coming from.

Cause of all Causes

God is the one and only. He gives life, and therefore no one can oppose Him. Then why are there circumstances that seem to oppose the kingdom of God? They are an illusion in the hearts of those who do not have true faith. But really, God is He Who makes all things happen.

Force of Faith

There are times when we are blessed with understanding and do God's will with logic. Other times, our heart and mind are closed and we must follow His directives by force of faith. By subordinating all parts of our life to spiritual understanding, we can then observe the commandments even without understanding.

Insane

A woman who, despite her husband's divorcing her, keeps returning to him, cannot be divorced. She is deemed insane, unable to accept a divorce with responsibility. Similarly, the Jewish people, as many times as they suffer exile and attempted annihilation, keep returning to God and wait by the gates till God has mercy on them. It is better to be thought insane than to be a sinner for even one instant. Even when their life is without spiritual sense, they do not search for answers from foreign sources.

Fear of God

Why is a king or government needed to protect the citizens? Because they lack the proper fear of God and respect for His creatures.

When we lack awe of God, where do we get it from? From the fear of man. We say, if we are ashamed of man then surely we ought to be ashamed of God?! It follows that if you fear God, you do not need to fear man.

The fear of kings of other nations helps one have fear of God's punishment. And the fear of Jewish kings gives us fear of His greatness.

Since the purpose of the king is merely to remind people about the fear of God, He must receive his power from the Torah. Then those in his presence feel the presence of the Torah through him. And if that does not help, then even the kings of other nations rule over us, and worse, even their servants do so.

Accessible

The more we clamor to be close to God, the more He makes Himself accessible.

Indirect Faith

One level of spiritual encounter is face to face, when God speaks to man directly, to one person or the entire generation. The other level is faith, when we receive the message indirectly, and that applies to anyone, anywhere, forever. One can bless only on his particular level, but can receive even if it is infinite.

Infinite Beginning

Just as God's first thought was of the Jewish people, so too they must surrender their first to Him. And when they do, then no mishap can ruin the last of it. God also re-establishes them as the first that they are.

Although an entire thing has measure, the beginning of it is infinite. And therefore if we are connected to the start of all things, we have the infinite part of it.

Despite It All

There is the truth of the truth, and there is faith. Faith is needed in time of confusion, in the darkness of exile or suffering. When one accepts the suffering, he is able to have faith despite it and to live.

God's Strength

The Jewish people are always happier to be weak themselves and receive all strength from God, than to have the strong hands of Esau the wicked one.

Joy or Pain

Just as one who is happy must rejoice with the Torah and the commandments more than any other joy, when he is in pain, he has to be pained by the lack of spiritual development more than any other pain. Either in joy or in pain, he can serve God.

Love God

Naturally all creatures are drawn to follow God. And if man is mindful and does not allow evil to overwhelm him, he too will follow in God's ways. And he will also love God, since he did not allow lust to overpower his love.

Start and End

We cannot start anything on our own and neither can we finish. Both need the help of God.

Loving Calls

The entire Torah consists of names of God in various combinations. Those who study it, expound it, and delve into its details and wisdom are all calling God's name. And the more often His name is called, the more intimate the caller gets with Him, and God responds in kind.

Like a Sheep

Often man wants to be his own boss, and many go to great lengths to show this. Yet the true servant of God is happier following God as a sheep follows his shepherd.

14

The Holy Land

Israel

There is the physical and the spiritual land, *Eretz Yisroel*. It is so named because the nation of Israel are the ones who have the vessels to appreciate it. Once they leave, all that is left is desert and desolation.

Small but Infinite

Eretz Yisroel is physically small but spiritually infinite.

Needed

The Jewish people need the land of Israel, and the land needs them, too.

Two Sides of the Coin

The greatest joy was to be in the presence of God, in the Holy Temple of our Holy Land. The destruction of the Temple and exile, however, caused crying, mourning, and yearning; two sides of the same coin.

Mirrors

God's material gifts have spiritual mirror images. The Holy Land, Jerusalem, and the Holy Temple are all physical, yet they exist in the spiritual realm, too. Therefore, although we may no longer have the physical portion, we still have the spiritual part just as before.

Ancestors' Merit

Even if the Jewish people have no merit to inherit the land of Israel, they have the merit of their ancestors.

Conduit

All providence and blessing received by other lands comes through the Holy Land.

Holy Land

Eating the fruit of *Eretz Yisroel* stimulates man's soul to praise and thank God. In addition, the holiness of the land and everything that grows on it is a blessing in itself.

Joy and Awe

In times and places of holiness, on the Sabbath or in the land of Israel, if one had joy he could experience awe of God. And where unholiness prevails, as on the weekdays and in the land of exile, with awe we can reach joy.

Holy Land

Geography and climate influence people, their lifestyle, and their habits. So too the spiritual features of places have similar influence on the spirits of men. This is why the land of Israel is especially conducive to spiritual growth and development. As promised to Abraham, the land of his inheritance will make his children, just as his children make the land.

15

Redemption from Exile

Within

The Jewish people have learned, since the time of their ancestors, to look for salvation within even in the tragedy itself.

At Rest

One can be immobile and in one place, yet his heart and mind are racing non-stop. On the other hand, one can be journeying from place to place and be at peace and at rest.

Darkness

We experience dark periods when God's kingdom is hidden. Although the divine, holy sparks are imprisoned, we are destined to gather and liberate them. And when we find God even in the worst situation, this is spiritually so profound that we can hardly hold on to it. We must strain till the new concept stays with us.

Lessons

We may pass through many dark periods, and surely there is something to learn from each one. But those lessons may be overlooked and ignored. We must therefore pause and reflect upon unpleasant, difficult, and tragic events. We must gain from them all there is to learn.

Redemption

There are three enslavers of man: the evil inclination, the evil side, and Satan. There are also three corresponding levels of redemption: daughter, then sister, then mother. When one arrives at the last level, one can accomplish his particular mission.

New Clarity

Just as there is new confusion and exile each day, there is also new clarity and redemption.

Great Enthusiasm

If one were to do even one single good deed completely, without the slightest reservation, and on the contrary with great enthusiasm and energy, it would ultimately lead to complete redemption.

Renewal

There is no renewal except God, the root of all renewal. The celestial creatures do not change and are therefore not renewed. It is only the creations that need constant renewal.

Keys

There are keys to the outside gates and keys to the inside gates. The first open the doors to bodily freedom; the second open the doors to spiritual freedom.

Accumulating Merit

The good deeds and merit of each generation accumulate till there is enough good to have the Holy Temple rebuilt.

God Remembers

When the Jewish people were in their land, *Eretz Yisroel*, and worshiped in the Holy Temple, they did not realize how good it was. And so we pray, "God, You know how good we had it. Please remember us!"

The King's Daughter

The knight who slays the dragon marries the king's daughter. Those who struggle with evil, and persevere to the end, will be rewarded with endless knowledge and understanding. They will find the fountainhead, the gates of the Torah, and drink its waters.

Lacking

The Exodus is a reminder that God is present even within the exile, and that is the redemption. And one who realizes that can pray to God, because all prayer serves to remove the concealment resulting from something lacking.

Lifting the Lowly

Man's mission in life is to lift up the holy sparks from their lowly exile. By realizing that there is no place where He is not found, you find the sparks and can relate to them. Everything that comes your way, even strange thoughts, present themselves only in order that you uplift them.

Receiving the Gift

Because Joshua received everything from Moses, he therefore led the Israelites into the Holy Land, which was a divine
gift to which the recipients did not contribute anything. And
anyone who wants to have a share in that land must negate
himself completely and accept it as a gift.

Man and Beast

Man has an animal nature and its bodily needs, and also a
spiritual nature and intellect. Man's body gets enslaved to its
needs and desires. He then prays from his exile and yearns
for redemption. When he is redeemed, he is finally able to
pray with his entire being. Man and beast will be helped by
God.

Earned Redemption

The redemption can come either as a gift from God, at its
proper time, or before its time as a result of our hard work.
God, however, has great joy if His providence is earned.

Trust in Good Times

It is difficult to trust in God's imminent help when we are in
trouble. But it is even harder to put our complete trust in Him,
and Him only, when our life is in order.

All for the Good

We believe with conviction that all the challenges, tests, pain, and suffering visited upon the Jewish people are, in the end, all for the good. They were chosen to establish, make known, and prove without a doubt, from the lowest to the highest spheres, that God is the one and only. The higher spiritual spheres are places of freedom and expanse, the lower ones places of enslavement and confinement. The higher spheres shine the light of His kingdom even into those murky dungeons, break the walls of enslavement, and expand the constriction to infinity.

Protected

The more holiness one reaches for and attains, the less evil can harm him. Thus during the week one will eat with great care, so as to rise above the physical aspect of the food. On the Sabbath, though, one is spiritually uplifted and the physical aspect of the food will be in harmony with him. [When the Messiah arrives, we will attain great spiritual heights allowing us to eat, even forbidden foods, without adversely affecting our development.]

Slave to Nature

Odom Horishon, Adam, belonged in the Garden of Eden. That amazing place was suited for his lofty spiritual level. After he sinned, he was expelled and worked the physical earth for his bread. He was a slave to nature. Yet even a freed slave must receive a gift from his master from each of his possessions. Man too, although working as a slave, received gifts from his Master. And man does, too.

Forbidden Food

The foods forbidden by the Torah have holy sparks that cannot be released. They are therefore called *maacholos asuros*, imprisoned foods, because they cause the spirit of man to be imprisoned. On the other hand, there is eating on the level of freedom, which liberates the spirit of man and causes it to soar. Actually we are always eating at the "table before God." Although it is hidden, with the Torah it is revealed to us.

Royal Family

With the Exodus the Israelites were transformed from slaves to servants of God. They were given power and charged with warding off the enemies of the kingdom. Then at Mount Sinai they were again changed, this time to children of God. Like a prince, they had the power to bring other nations into the royal circle.

Help Yourself

To the extent that one helps another and lightens his burden, his own burden lightens, and he is able to bear it.

Learning to Speak

When the Israelites were liberated from Egyptian slavery, they were like a newborn babe who soon learns to speak. The first thing you teach a baby to say is, "The Torah was commanded to us by Moses. It is an inheritance to the congregations of Jacob." Similarly, each time we renew our life with repentance we too must immediately learn to speak words of Torah.

Always with Joy

Just as the exile is a result of not serving God with joy, if we do so serve Him, then the gates of redemption open. One needs to rejoice in the service of God more than in all the pleasures of the world. That way we lose neither the joy nor the riches. As it is written, whoever observes the Torah in poverty will observe it later in riches; and whoever does not observe it in riches will not observe it later in poverty.

The Prince

The *Zohar* teaches, "A prince was sent to a village to learn firsthand of the effects of his father's kingdom. When he grew up, his father sent for him to return to the palace. The villagers were very upset and cried. A wise man among them said, 'Why are you upset? Is he not a prince, who belongs in the palace?'"

Man is also a prince, a son of God, sent from heaven to learn the workings of the Kingdom of God. That son, the soul, is imprisoned within the body, which is merely a servant. And its goal is, in the end, to return to the palace of the King.

Index

ABOUT THE AUTHOR

Moshe A. Braun is the director of Hope Educational Services, providing communities with educational innovations. He also directs the Free Jewish University, a Torah outreach program for college age youth. (*sic*) A Holocaust survivor who has written and lectured on the subject at college campuses, he is also one of the pioneers in popularizing hasidic ideas through lectures and published articles. Braun has written more than ten books, including *The Talking Bsomim Box* (1990), *Leap of Faith* (1992), *The Magic Comb* (1993), *The Jewish Holy Days* (1996), *Pointing the Way: Spiritual Insights from Sfas Emes* (1997), *The Heschel Tradition: The Life and Teachings of Rabbi Abraham Joshua Heschel of Apt* (1997), and *Sabbath Peace: A Book of Meditations* (1997). He resides in New York with his wife and children.